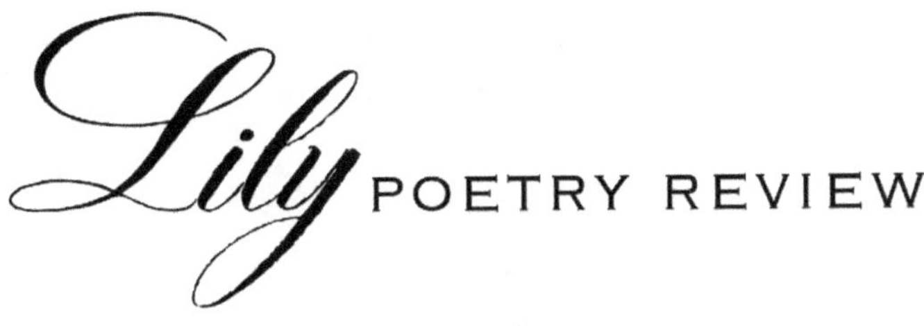

ISSUE 13

*Dedicated to the memory
of Karen Friedland,1963-2024*

EDITOR-IN-CHIEF
Eileen Cleary

ASSISTANT EDITOR
Mark Walsh

ASSOCIATE EDITOR
Christine Jones

ART EDITOR
Lisa Sullivan

BOOK REVIEW EDITOR
Amanda Shaw

VISPO EDITOR
Suzanne Mercury

WEB EDITOR
Rebecca Connors

MEDIA AND EVENTS
Frances Donovan

READERS
Susan Kay Anderson, Jules Jacob,
K. T. Landon, Michelle Lynch, Gloria Monaghan,
Tzynya Pinchback, Sarah Dickenson Snyder,
Anastasia Vassos

DESIGN
Martha McCollough

COVER ART, ISSUE 13
Susan Solomon, detail from "Puffin"

Letter from the Editors

Dear Readers,

Whether you hold as a contributor or reader, we are grateful to have you as part of *Lily*. We wouldn't be where we are without you, or our over 800 contributors thus far, or our dedicated and talented team of volunteers.

This issue opens with "Crow Wonders What It's Like to Be a Poet" by Peter Grandbois who reflects upon how poetry translates a "world that is always, already/ here, in a language no one knows, and/ there it is, the thing, now a bowl//A singing bowl, asking to be filled." We take this opportunity to remember two poets who have recently died, Karen Friedland and Martha Silano. We mourn that there are two fewer translators of the world waiting to be written. The issue includes a sketch of Karen Friedland contributed by the artist Peter Urkowitz. Friedland had also submitted two of her poems to this issue. Her poems are followed by "Forsythia x intermedia," an elegy for Friedland written by Anastasia Vassos. We also invite you to read Kathleen Flenniken's review of *This One We Call Ours* by Martha Silano (Lynx House Press, 2024.)

We share this beautiful and accomplished work in joy and hope.

Sincerely,
Eileen Cleary

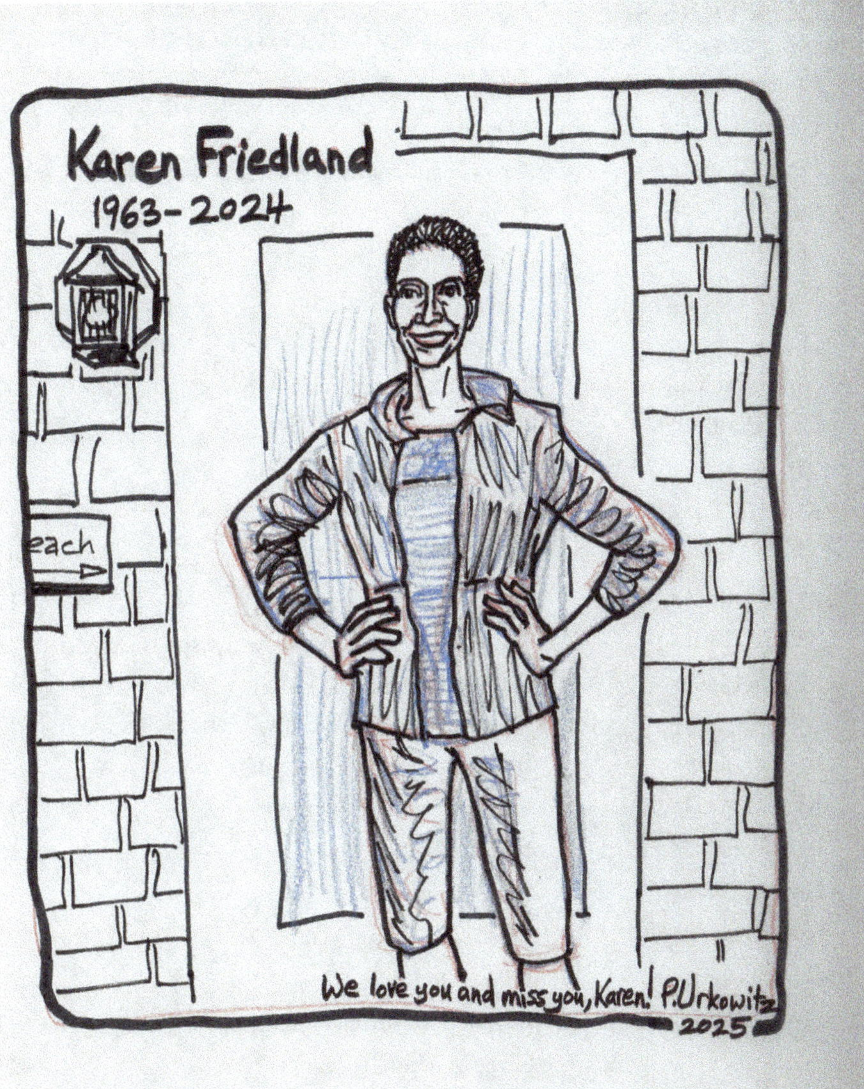

Karen Friedland
1963 - 2024
each
We love you and miss you, Karen! P. Urkowitz
2025

CONTENTS

Book Reviews:

PETER GRANDBOIS

Crow wonders what it's like to be a poet

Nevertheless, the rain continues, dark as
a ragged child, wandering a road without end,
mist rising, obscuring the numberless dead

Nevertheless, the child, a girl, drops something
as she passes through a muddy field,
a small thing, something she'll never miss

So it is here, with this accident, that our dull eyes
turn toward . . . what refuge, what beauteous disaster?
The field is filled only with what we cannot see

Nevertheless, the rain. The field. The mud
vibrates with our humming, a lullaby
to which we've forgotten the words

Making a world that is always, already
here, in a language no one knows, and
there it is, the thing, now a bowl

A singing bowl, asking to be filled

STEVE FAY

Deletion

The breath leaving the threadbare daybed, as it's carried to the front
    stoop.
The red-faced draymen waiting in the street to carry it away.

The old man protesting from the parlor window.
Unheard, as if his tongue was broken or was somehow tangled inside
    of a chunk of potato.

One wing of the eagle, on the badge certifying the draymen's cart,
    seeming to have lengthened, but it is only dried schmutz that
    had dripped from some other refuse they have carried.
A chunk of asphalt adheres to one of their mule's hind hooves, but it
    is more ignorable to the mule than the green fly worrying its
    left ear.

The old man's daughter hands over a jar of homemade pickles and
    some smoked carp wrapped in paper.
The older drayman's grin betrays his broken teeth, as he accepts their
    payment.

Inside, the old man startles at the boxes newly packed with his
    clothes, his keepsakes, his holy icons, the unlit lamp.
As dusk arrives, light from the drawbridge down the street begins to
    flicker inside his apartment.

In near darkness, the old man frantically points to the walls, his
    mouth ajar, as if he recalls something hidden behind the
    plaster.
Outside, the line of carts and people stops, waits while traffic on the
    canal continues to pass.

JED MYERS

To a Younger Poet
—for Erin

Thought of you as I wove through the giants—
battered old firs, towers poked full of dark
alcoves by beetles and birds—

along a creek edged with silver ice,
toward the lake. And so many monsters lay
dead, thick torsos bent limp

on the ground's contours, saplings
risen through the moss shrouds. Thought
of you again at the lake's shore, mirror

banks offered down to a harbor
of cloud. Heard myself murmur
We can't be in that world of no word,

no story. The lake valley won't write
its own few lines on the crash of the next
immense conifer, won't praise

the fungal-and-rot savor of death's
local nectars, won't rhyme to the trickle-
cadence of crystal-encased fern tips….

We're the ones who'll twitch and bristle
with dread and thrill, itching to scrawl.
We're the enthralled interpreters,

letters like black blood in our fingers
pressing to spill. And troubled enough
by lessened light to turn back, on the path

I passed a great tall trunk, apartments
carved in its ridged wall—in one shadow
a bird flinched. I thought, might live the night.

KAREN FRIEDLAND
Thank You, Neighbors

-

For letting your wind-blown trees grow big,
for planting "succession" gardens,
that blossom all summer long,

for cooking dinners
that waft from open windows,
for practicing pianos by them, too.

Thank you for your concern and care
about my incurable, inoperable cancer,
not unlike the fatal cancers of past neighbors—

Goodbye, Jeanette,
farewell, "Angel"—
both dead of lady cancers
much like mine.

All of us decent sorts
who waved and said hi,
all of us sad to see each other die.

KAREN FRIEDLAND

A Decent Scan

I don't want to get cocky
in my aliveness—
after all, my eyelashes have just fallen out,
and this thing *will* kill me—

But a glimmer of hope is a beautiful thing—
the largest tumor on my liver
up and disappeared!

allowing me more time
to listen to evening crickets—

a late-season's sermon
on everything's excellence.

ANASTASIA VASSOS

Forsythia x intermedia
—for Karen Friedland

 I knew you would stay until spring.

Dead sounded different once: the cloistered crypt,
faraway laughter.

Wicker filled with ash of you.

A basket tosses my high-mourn loss, the petals torn
from roses, trowel of dirt,

thud of clay, and you, Soul-girl, gone.

A longing, a lengthening. Hints of forsythia.
Log-bones in leafing grass.

Such grave-step resurgence. In particular, spring.
Something in between

in periphery, erratic pansies. The sky's blistering bulb,
clouds' collective incandescence.

The cure for sorrow is my living body.
I cannot say if you hear the geese overhead.

DAISY KULINA

Ritual

My father in love
with a hayfield fuller than last year,
winter oranges, and timely first snows:
all *for the health of the barns,*
he has insisted since the day

he found the structures *perishing*
like the meat chickens we kept as pets,
plucked to the flesh only by time.

Each year, he nurses
those barns back to health,
arms them with a new layer of red paint
to take a stand against the sun.

There are things I have learned
to treasure: liquor and heat lamps
and early March because *you should never
run from what keeps you warm.*

Nothing to love more
than the ins and outs of sunlight
as it explores elderly roofing,
the livelihood of deceased livestock
that coats the walls, runs
to the floor in a thick salt.

DAISY KULINA

we grew up in the bitterroot

when august kisses the top of blue mountain
the river girls dance cinnamon dances
submit to the exhaustive showers

some with cracked hair, some cracked
throats this is how it feels to unknowingly
suffocate in the warmer colors, the fiercer
time of year

the shrinking inside sank them
through the pine & pain
to river bottom

body's bed resting nested
another body
she calls them in rasp & river water

earthy uncomfort embraced
when it was tradition
but now she just seeps

if pores were pipes
a riverbed for the river girls
swallowing, swallowing

when the river's wide mouth was tamed
everyone loved it
body in body on body.

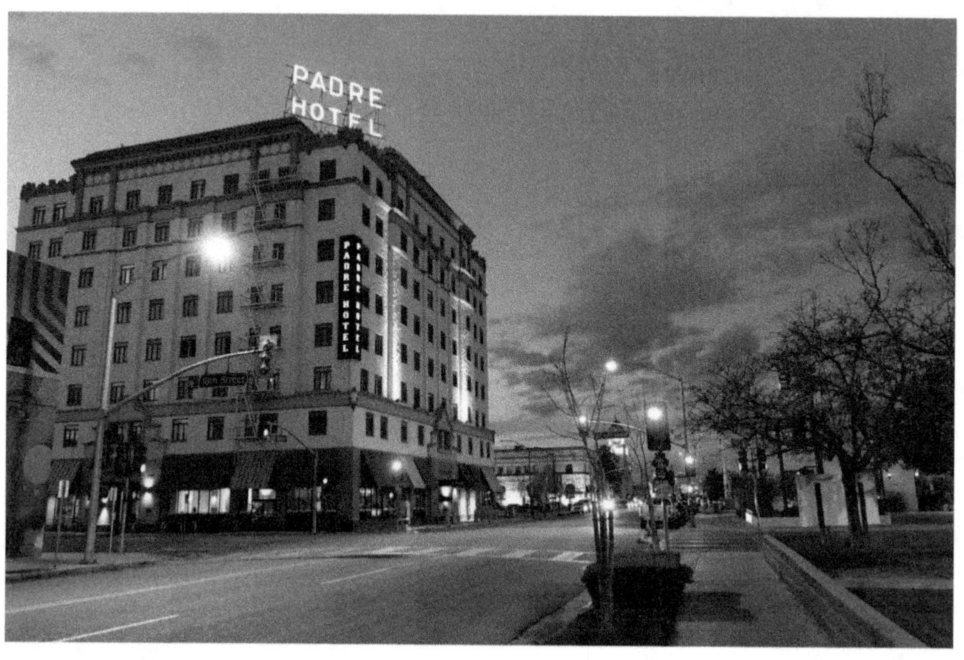
PADRE
HOTEL
PADRE HOTEL

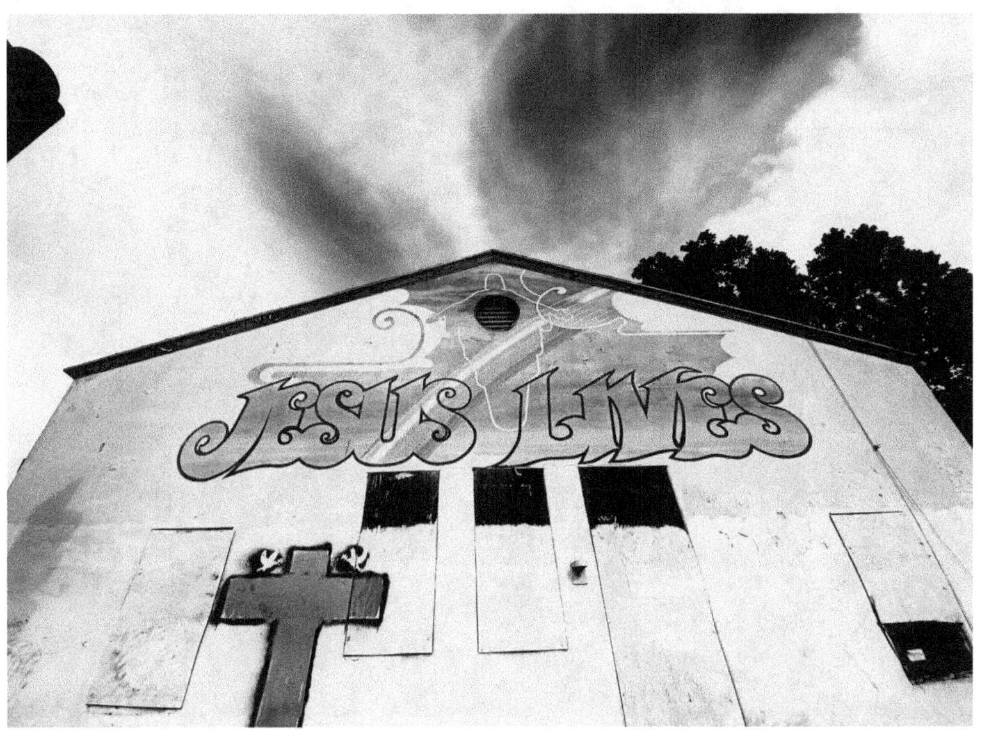
JESUS LIVES

Manzanar Afternoon

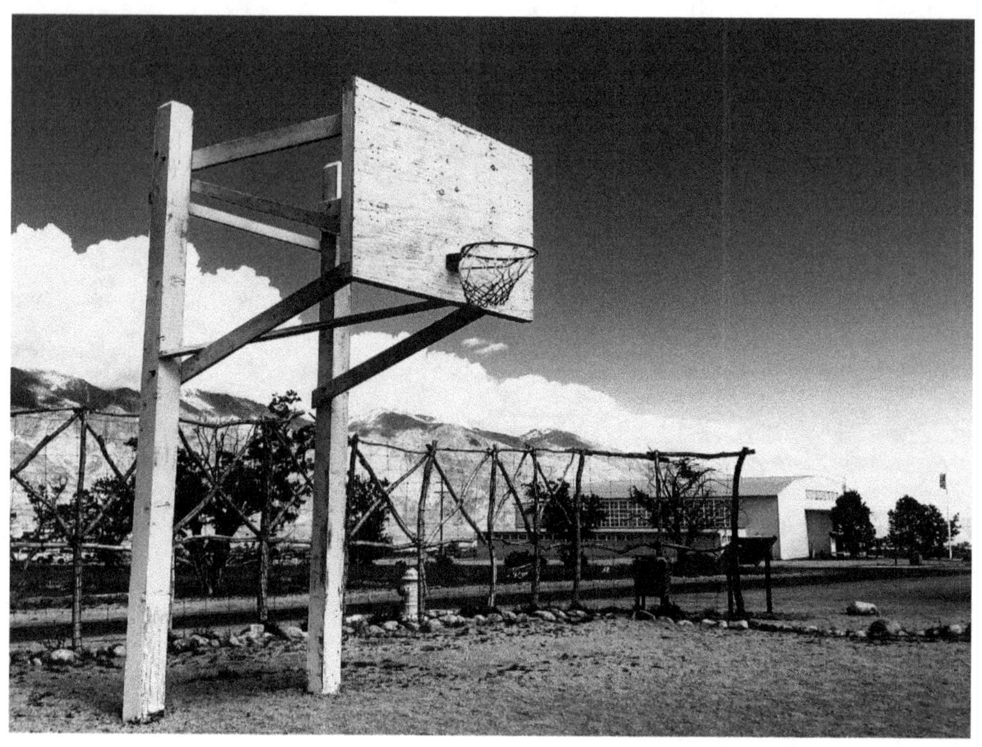

STELIOS MORMORIS

Conchita makes ceviche when she is livid,

guts the cans of corn

with the spear-side of a bottle opener,

braises kernels black

as rotten teeth, then pours them

into lime ceramic bowls,

gnashed among the fleshy cubes

of runny tomato embedded with seeds

translucent as x-rays.

She throws choruses

of thyme—ridged spears littering the mix

to calm the heart awry—

scallions scattered everywhere,

lithe green tubes blanched as shocked

eyes upon the cutting and toss,

olive oil lubricating the whole mess.

She manages a flash

of smile in her storm of a rumba

whisking up a white beach

with a swivel of hip,

holding back a horizon of tears

but shakes the salt anyway, like a maraca,

then taps a brief rain of pepper.

Drawers clang shut

with mismatched forks and spoons.

Conchita sings about a poisonous rose,

and splays a fan of sweating

crescents of avocado

atop the heap—this varietal hive

of edible flesh brimming with light.

MICHAEL JONES

Mt. Diablo's Bright Valley & Shadowed Summit, Seen From The Freeway

Caminante, no hay camino, / el camino se hace al andar. – Machado

Backlit storm fringe, clarion clearing:
the road I'm on crosses the continent.

Clouds whose shifting confounds foundation:
teach me how walking can make a way.

ROGER CAMP

Breakfast on the square in Vilnius

I watch the taxis jockey

      like ducklings streaming after mother

in front of the hotel restaurant.

Its double paned windows

      strangling noise into a dumb show.

The pedestrian crowd

births a bicycle, the front tire

   wobbling like a dropped foal, a satchel

of school books bouncing from the handlebars.

Vigorously pedaled by a young father,

   his daughter straddles the rear carrier

her hands clutching his ballooning back pockets.

Oblivious to the bike's erratic path,

   she leans back confident,

beatific face angled skyward,

carefree, tilted just enough

   for me to see.

Joy drowns me.

KRISTIN W. DAVIS

Victim Impact Statement

The weeping cherry in our garden, the one we call the Amy Tree, is in full bloom the day Amy's
 murderer is up for parole. At sunrise, delicate blossoms, coral-gold. An hour later, each fluff of pink
a gasp in the gray light.

The rest of my family will travel hundreds of miles—enter the prison without
a bottle of water or stick of gum—to look him in the eye, speak of the numb weight of grief. He will
stare ahead. Not in their direction.

I cannot make this pilgrimage of testimony. In writing, I name the perseverance of ache. I cannot
summon a desire to stare down, to squint in rebuke. This is no flutter of forgiveness.

It is the dead place—he knows it, too—
where nothing so vital as fury will blossom.

JENNY GRASSL

How to Grow Cover

I.

daffodils break stare

body newfangle

I spy a stag through branches

throw wish at his feet

nearing—being—

deer—

how a woman crowned for the hunt   too naked for snow bed—

lance and saw-tooth flake

split arcs of storm

I have left the dining room

to land here on four hooves   a stammer

II.

mating   remembered as late summer

                    how in his yard how a freeze

near death

          how an elder silver doe brings attar of com-

pass rose

                    one drink in spring and I belong

CRAIG DOBSON

Spring Fox

They shot him between daffodil fade and bluebell prime.

Left him near the field gate – his brush towards the lane,

his snout to the nearby lambs beneath the waking oak

and, beyond that, the new-ploughed hill

whose crest was bright with yellow tape.

He was still perfect, a resting death in the year's new green.

Crows, I guess, took the first red and grey tufts, littering the grass.

Next, a dozen bluebottles, fat with purpose, busy round his harmless snarl.

By first red campion, he stank from yards away;

grown dull, he wore maggots at his opened throat.

Bald grey skin showed more the collapse within.

Why leave him, where the wind now decides him –

how he waits and shifts among the lambs and along the lane, fouling the air?

Why leave him there?

SETH ROSENBLOOM

There Is a Dying Wolf

I know him. Mangy, half-starved. The throb
of his blood is warm next to mine. The howl
from his last kill arcs the muscles of my mouth.

In the end, Villagers come. Their torches lick
the night. Shepherds good to slaughter a beast
hungry for one of the flock.

Swing the axe at the throat that guards the den.
Smoke out the mother and her pups, herd
their moans into the fire.

And I am telling you this because I don't want
the wolf to die. Yet, thank God he is too weak
to lunge at new flesh.

In 1,000 years, people will still search its eyes
and argue who's inside who.

But what I want you to know is this.
There is a dying wolf and he and you are close.

CYNTHIA BARGAR

Pillow Dogs

Every night & all night long
dogs romp my pillow, my greedy sleep.

Rhodesian Ridgeback & Weimaraner
vie for each dream, jaws & teeth.

> Savage bed sentries
>
> they eviscerate rattlesnakes
>
> coiling my ankles.

Dogs that preserve me for heaven,
dogs that float me in champagne bubbles,
scrub me lavender, & cucumber my eyes.

Watch out for the serial killer lurking in my kitchen
knife in hand unaware of you, my pillow dogs —
> your fierce devotion.

MARCI RAE JOHNSON

Instructions for Decapitation

Dogen's Rules for Zazen, *in the eleventh month,*
first year of Kangen [1243], with My Little Pony

Set aside all involvements and let the ponies rest.
A *quiet place is suitable.* Contemplate
their rainbow manes. The large eyes, each

with a dewdrop inside—the whole moon reflected.
Do not desire to pop the head from the neck just yet.

Be mindful of the passing of time—each moment
a mountain, the ponies' eyes a disguise for where

the poem wants to take you. *It is not*

a conscious endeavor. The colors remind you of spring,
which is only spring—not a sign
of what's to come—summer, the lush

green and gold, getting drunk on the apricot sun.
You would grow old on the flat stone
where we're holding hands with the lightest

of touch, waiting for silence to envelop us.
Protect and maintain the place where you settle
your body, under the one tree visible above

the stone wall. *Loosen your robes.*
Let the old desires fade away—the need
to destroy in order to create. Instead,

with the hands in this position, place them beside
your body, eyes open.

TOBI ALFIER

Slices of Mae

I.

White polka-dots on cute red dress

from the sample rack at the *Here and There*

with cleavage just enough for sunglasses

and a hanky. You never know when

those tears will be coming, black stripes

down your face make everything worse.

 On barstools you share judgements

of the world, and of yourself, with strangers,

and you are tired of bickering, bickering, bickering.

You tilt down the rest of your watered down

Cuba Libre, call a couple girlfriends

to meet you at the casino, and glide off

gracefully, leaving a salute of surrender

in your wake. You grab a room, for how long

you don't know, wash your panties, look through

your purse for cash, credit and lipstick, and wait

in your oasis with walls so thin you feel like a voyeur,

hope there'll be no bickering from that direction.

II.

Your room looks like a clothing world exploded.

You borrow a pair of black tights from 1972

and a brilliantly sheer blouse with flowers

and tiny birds like the ones living

under the eaves of your house. You feel free

as you climb into the elevator with your friends.

You all go to dinner. At the fancy restaurant.

Order Kir Royals and *Ladie's Cut* Prime Rib,

play Keno, lose at Keno, play again and have dessert.

It's too early to turn in and count sheep, you all agree.

No snide remarks at dinner, no bickering over men, money,

the bill—you charge it to the room pretty as you please.

You play the slots, flirt with the bartenders,

watch a bride play Blackjack out of the corner

of your eye. She's still in her dress with hair gone rogue,

7-month belly hiding under the table,

a pile of chips in front and a full ashtray beside her,

the groom nowhere to be seen, just like yours.

III.

A few moans as faces appear like petals

dropped from a weak morning sun,

except Ava, purse and shoes missing.

She might've headed off home to her man

or found a newer one, who knows.

You need food, oh lord, you need something.

You all stumble into the elevator in last night's clothes

stinking of cigarettes and dirty quarters, but jubilant

at your two-day escape—all your friends needed it, 100 percent.

The elevator air is stained with other people's ardor.

You don't have to slave over breakfast for a change

but you're mindful that this is your last day.

The cook's name is Chase. You watch him watch you

through the window. A blink of an eye and he's there,

next to you, slice of pound cake tucked into your purse, a bribe.

You tell him you're married. Very married. He shrugs.

You blush at the drowsy tempo of his insinuation/invitation but no,

that's just not you. You eat the pound cake on the way home.

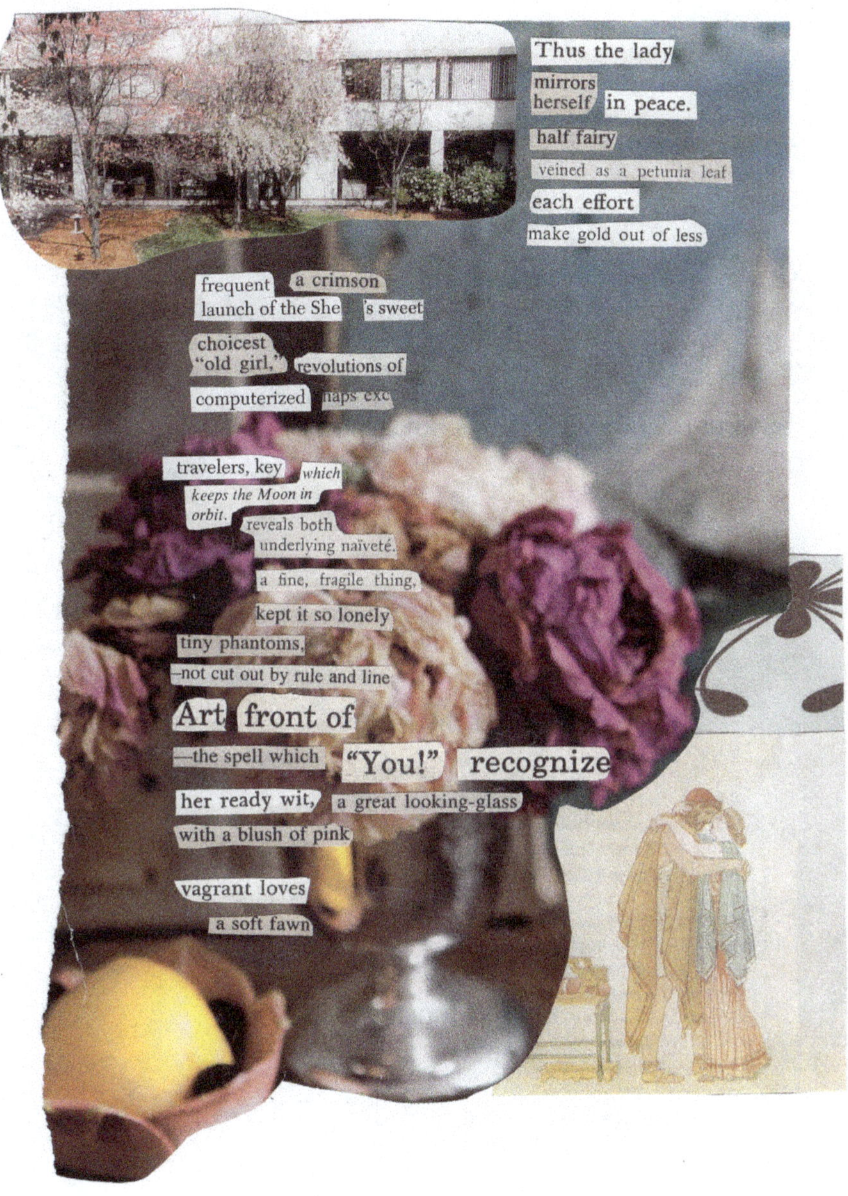
Thus the lady
mirrors
herself in peace.
half fairy
veined as a petunia leaf
each effort
make gold out of less
frequent a crimson
launch of the She 's sweet
choicest
"old girl," revolutions of
computerized naps exc
travelers, key which
keeps the Moon in
orbit. reveals both
underlying naïveté.
a fine, fragile thing,
kept it so lonely
tiny phantoms,
—not cut out by rule and line
Art front of
—the spell which "You!" recognize
her ready wit, a great looking-glass
with a blush of pink
vagrant loves
a soft fawn

Deadly to Appear

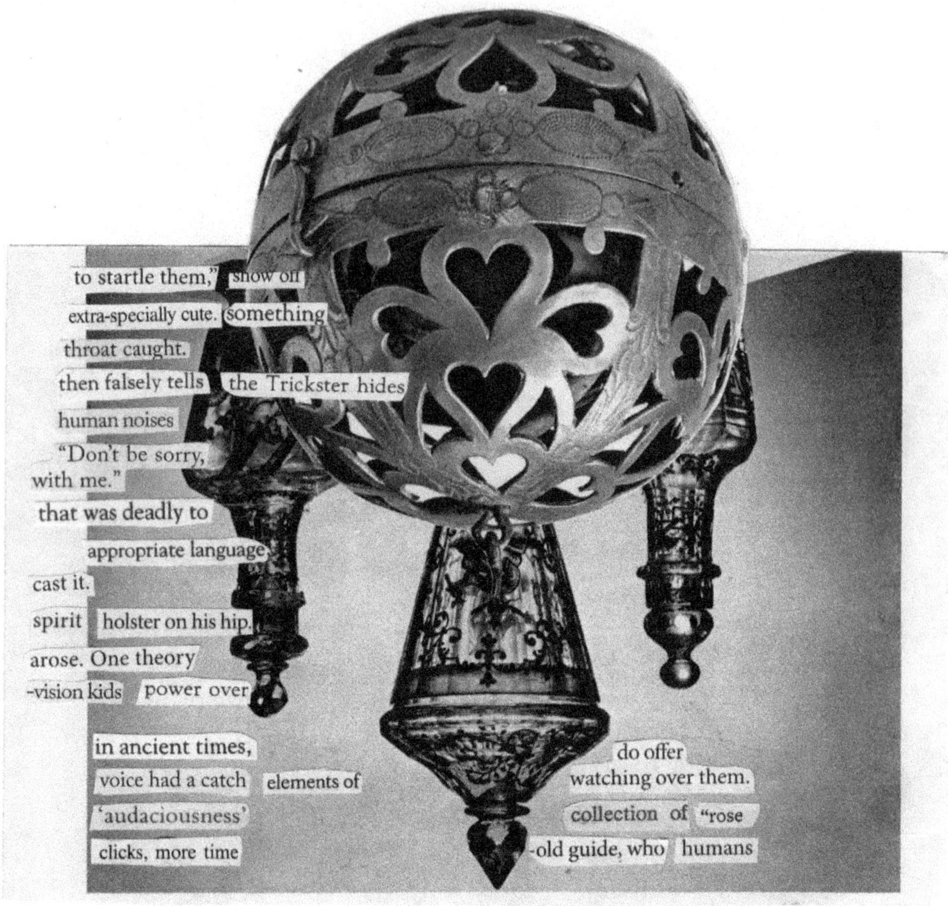

Do the Spell(ing)

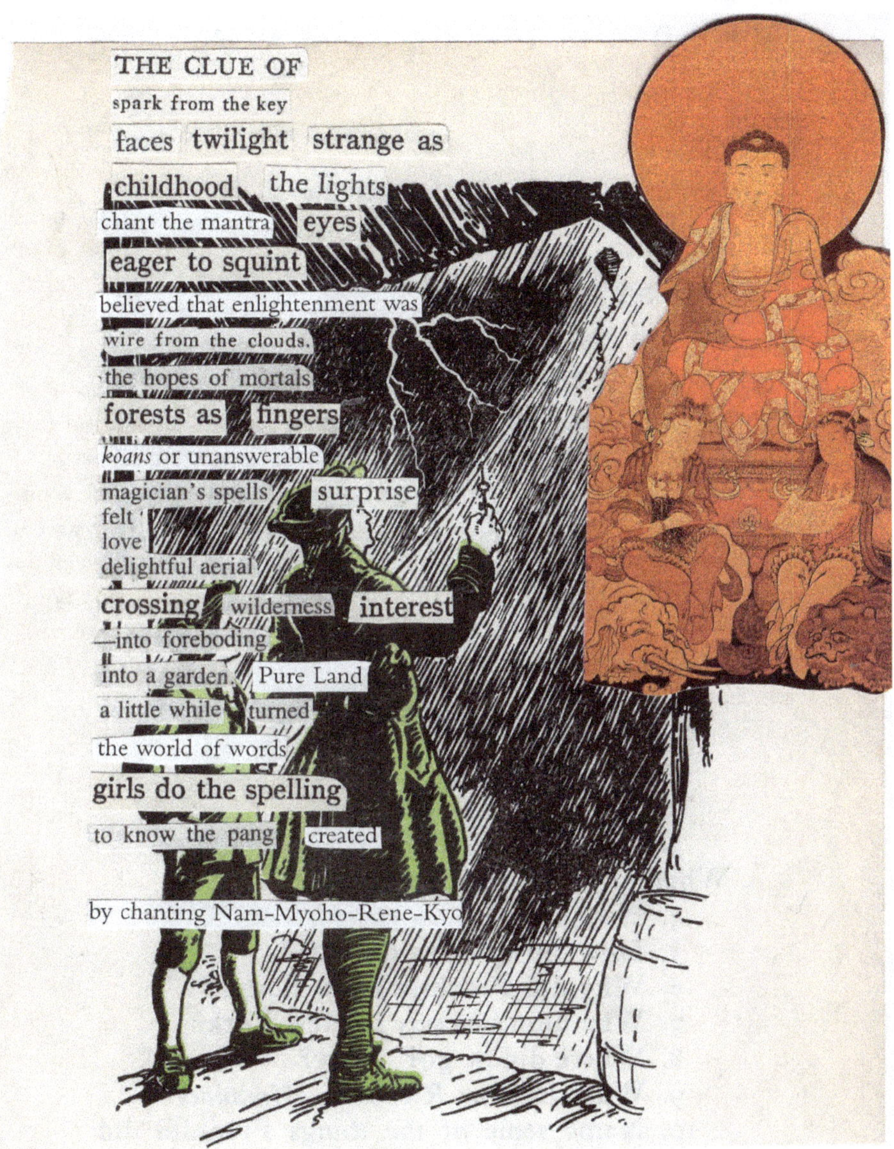

MARGO BERDESHEVSKY

OF MIND

> *The country where he lives/ is haunted/ by the ghost of an old forest.*
> *—Wendell Berry*

Prayer, after forgetting how or even what it is — is— A *mind*, haunted
by waking. Rises from wet leaf fall, call it winter's detritus, call it loam
or soil for the first-again sprout, call it thought-dust ... call it ... land
of afterwards, breeze-bright — its mere hum, and call it food sipped
in the womb-blood, for a kiss, heard in some cradle — but call it seed.
Mind, you say? It's no larger than a fist or a toadstool but fairy-home of
all our cries : How does the owl fly, how does the storm kill or a star-fall
end? *Mind*, you say, what symphony is it? *Mind,* what are its prayers,
how does it desire, does it desire? ... sheathed in nerves and blue veins
and bone, is it more like a turtle, a wing, a newborn ... or heavy as a
war's howl? And yes, say it because it is also true ...deadly... even in
the beds of lust. Say "Were you thinking of me, darling? Do you hope
I am at peace, are you at one with me and can we speak as roots do,
to ... say...love?" *Mind.* After forgetting prayer — is it the soil of the
monster or child-maker or a yellow sprout in its dream-wet earth ... is
it spring "haunted by the ghost of an old forest....." ?   darling
?

KRISTEN HEWITT

Bird Law

1.

Let them figure it out.

Let them use their beaks.

      Help no one.

As in an old stone bridge,

the blocks wedge tighter together

with weight from above—

but the keystone,

if pressed up from beneath,

collapses the whole.

2.

A berry: a single fleshy fruit

without a stone.

I didn't step

on any of them.

3.

The words in yellow

spray paint are an old spell.

Residual. Commandment.

Bird Law.

4.

Everyone has their rules,

electric fences they know

better than to cross.

You watch with horror

and desire as they

stop short, contorting,

as if up against a wall.

5.

The early bird—

a puritan story

we like to tell.

Bottom dwellers

make another mark

on the world.

6.

The witchcraft literature

is thick with toads—

a certain wet density.

Disloyal and quick

to cheat the neighbor,

steal a cow,

or light a fire.

7.

The worms are said

not to suffer,

exhibit no preference

for being

      cut in half

(or not).

They do not resist—

they do not desire—

and yet come up from the earth

      when it rains.

8.

The cowbird holds

her secret labor

in your nest. She

requires your assistance.

You will love her children

before you know

what you have done,

what rules you have broken.

COLIN JEFFREY MORRIS

Background Before Bird

Audubon often painted directly onto flora and landscapes composed by assistants.

The absolute blue of the *Yellow Rail*

sky is leached through by a dark

reach of grasses.

A prefigured stem shows through

Northern Parula – a diaphane

lit on a frame.

A curlicue shoot of *franklinia*

shows through *Bachman's Warbler*

(extinct). The bird-forms are flat,

formulaic, surrendering all

to the leaves.

MARY MORRIS

Postcard, Marrakesh, 4 a.m.

Dark street.

Scent of saffron.

Nighthawk flies above

strum of an oud.

Twelfth century mosque.

An empty souk.

PAM DAVENPORT

Indefinite Article

A cement and exposed brick wall, it crumbles around our eggs and coffee. *You know what to do,* she says.

A rock says *breathe,* says *grow,* and *you are.* But you think of Kfar Aza, of Derna, of Herat.

A bronze hand beckons from a photo. You could lie on the floor, crouch like a cat.

You are true to a word. This word. And the last and the next—

ROBBIE GAMBLE

To a Favorite Aunt

a good soul dissipates
and we are left with a tinge

of attic dust
on the tongue

the library shuttered or sold
with all its great volumes

a fog bank reluctantly settles
the tide is neap

this world, this world, how it dazzles
and you, you always listened

MIRIAM O'NEAL

In Possession of Family

All that spring and summer you kept notes:
This is what he said—what he did not say—
What the doctors said about him—how his feet spoke
beneath the sheet that last morning.

In between practicing translation, you spent your ink
to record his dying.   In Italian
possessive nouns of place use articles—
la mia casa, la mia stanza— the my house, the my room

(though in English we don't say *the*).
But in possession of family we say
mio fratello,   *my brother,*
no article of indication,   just   *my.*

The bag of his papers in your guestroom closet
tells fairytales, un-truths—*C'era una volta, Once upon a time,*
forms half-filled out: How often do you consume
alcohol?   *Only on weekends.   Solo nei fine settimana.*

And one day you wrote, *His dying has sockets*
and keys—ways to unlock my heart

if I can stand it—as if facing that door

weren't hard enough.   *Forza* means *strength.*

Ho così poca forza—*I have such little strength.*

The *r* rolls on the tongue, the *z* stops the rolling.

He liked to say *com si, com sa,*

as if saying something bluesy or romantic.

And though it was really gibberish, you knew he meant

It comes, it goes, this life or more to the point, *You lose, you lose again.*

Last night, so many months later, you heard his voice

inside your sister's voice as she wept. The way you heard

mountain snow-melt gushing in the Trevi

as water rained on itself—a voice all waters share,

submerged, subsumed, or flowing freely—

his baritone inside her soprano.

You had been learning to use the verbs *to open* & *to feel,*

adding adjectives as you practiced *we.*

You said, *Stasera apriamo tutte le finestre,*

  Tonight let's open all the windows

e sentiamo il bel vento—

  and feel the beautiful wind.

SUSAN JACKSON

The Changing Light Through the Window

My friend's son made her a gift of windows

      so from her sick bed upstairs

she could look out over the river behind her house,

      watch the blue heron swoop to fish along the bank

and across the bridge to her studio where she used to paint peonies

and lilacs,

      the waterfall, portraits of children with wide open faces.

Once in Switzerland we hiked half way up a mountain

      and paused on a bench along the path,

the sound of cow bells closer and closer and soon

      the hot breath of cows upon us… a herd on its way home for

milking,

she and I on a hillside in the dominion of friendship,

      sun and shadow over the green patches

of land as far as we could see. Could I have thought that's how

      death comes, with jangling bells and plodding hooves?

This evening her hand shapes the sheet hem as she sleeps.

      My body sinks further into the chair…

the changing light through the window… the words of Milosz

      You who I could not save Listen to me…

In the ancestral lands of northern Finland some say

      when a Sami dies they become rain.

I look out this evening at the dark clouds gathering

      in the western sky and imagine being rain…

rain that quenches plants and trees, nourishes the living things,

      invisible until it begins falling.

ANN QUINN

[Today the tree's ghostly shadows]

Today the tree's ghostly shadows

in the river and I

breathe in that reminder of death

Once I

looked in the mirror and glimpsed

from the corner of my eye

my mother long gone

What I

miss: being a daughter

encouraged to be an I

the "daughter"

but a trace — this short piece this I

a shadow of all that will ever be

Still this fear this "I"

must die for union

for annihilation of the I

CAITLIN T.D. ROBINSON

Is this your first?

she asks. When you lie down for your ER CT scan

after two hours of not knowing   *sit by the maskless woman's cough?*

stand by the opening and closing door?   strained swollen feet, one fractured

you don't know what to say

So you lie there, in short breaths

flatter than you want, stopping and starting gasps when asked

You try not to think about the form you signed   *the risks*

on a fetus are minimal   can't let it remind you of *the less than*   *risk losing*

a fetus after 14 weeks

how you did a year ago—just buildings away

the belly still   this time   full and wiggling.

Her first birthday, if she'd been punctual, would have been yesterday.

SUBHAGA CRYSTAL BACON

Weeks Before the Writing Conference

Does it matter that I dreamed this?

Womb, like a two-dimensional wall,

falls, becomes a door to a glacier

calving, open to another world.

And poems writing and revising

themselves? I'm afraid of being

alone in big crowds. I've always

found it hard to make and keep friends.

People calve from me—too cool to love—

safe to admire from a boat, or a door.

A womb empty of anything

but itself, cold, ragged, hidden

within fjords. Lines crossed,

then crossed out.

STEVEN OSTROWSKI

Experiment Days

It's necessity. We can't sit still, our hands are birds. We want to make
everything new and watch what we make fly toward original light.
We hear songs in spinning atoms. The gourmet world within mar-
inates flavors in our brains. A little frightened, we patrol the unlit
corridors of our personal history. We firmly believe in our doubts. We
try hard to make things swirl upward into that great open mouth that
speaks the holiest of the profane words. We chase the sun as it falls,
pens and brushes in hand, ready for everything a human being can
be ready for, which, granted, isn't much. That's okay: what we most
love is what we least understand. Days of hard nights in wordflow or
brushstroke, trials of harmony in painted stories, the whole grand
larceny of ideas that we're guilty of wanting too much. We become
artists in stillness after apprenticing in the blaring cacophony of the
daily grind. We refuse the half-life of ordinary time and ordinary
place on the grounds that it would bury us under-expressed, erased
before our own eyes, lost in malls and on laptop screens, consuming
our tales. In these experiment days, we thrive to fail, our pounding
hearts feel more than their fair share, we shout out beautiful nonsense
and somehow it makes sense anyway as it leaves our throats, because
we *mean* it and the universe understands, and like it, we offer the
sound of our words through years of dark and light so that they might
reach the strange kindness of any human ear.

BRIAN MOSHER

Shelter

library art gallery

a dank weekend afternoon

two without homes

in from the rain

with eleven laureates

as tobacco-scented

clothes and bones dry out,

are their hearts sheltered by the verse?

LINDA RAVENSWOOD

Leaving Gaza with a white flag

(a golden shovel)

Have you seen Rami Abu Jamous's film of his family leaving Gaza with white flags
made of bath towels? In the streets he walks with his camera on. He sees a neighbour ahead
also trying to leave. It is Abu Achmed and his boy on the sidewalk, also with white flags.
Rami calls out *Abu Achmed!* (Abu Achmed is crying.)
His son lies on cement, turned on his face, long and full of colours like a bull in the sand after a ritual. On
the pavement Abu Achmed is rolling and crying. Rami films. Abu Achmed cries
kan yanbaghi lana 'an nabqaa fi almanzil كان ينبغي لنا أن نبقى في المنزل
which means we should have stayed home in Arabic.
All are in prayer. He cries a hundred times. Suddenly they shout
yatanafas يتنفس *he breathes!* Abu Achmed lifts up
his son to carry him away. Another strong man comes to help.
Running in the streets, he holds the boy upon his arms.
Then a reporter says in English *the son of Abu Achmed did not live*
Finally his name is said. *Achmed Al Atbash.* CNN says *here are drone coordinates of the family*
as they fled. They show how they went from their flat
and the brief minutes it took to go around corners under
evacuation. They did not have guns, only broomstick and towel, and a plastic sack.
Rami films. A man on the road says *Gaza est tombé*
in French. It means the city has fallen

ELI SLOVER

Digging

The dead do not bury themselves.
    —Archaeologists' Creed

I should be elsewhere, but I have spent the
early night hours walking over leaves dead
and scattered on late November ground. I do
not think the moon shines full tonight and not
because the rushing clouds intend to bury
any indivisible light within themselves.

KATHY SHORR

Letter to a Friend in Tel Aviv

for Amelia Anisovych and in memory of Alisa Perebyinis

Last time we met was in a park.

The grass held you, half lounging,

propped on an elbow, hands free

to peel a mango in the sun.

Tell me, is your gun still hidden

on the roof? Did you keep

your government-issue gas mask?

It's been years, but I still keep you

in my head. Have you seen

this photo from Irpin: a just-

killed girl, Alisa, age 9,

whose body rests against a slushy

pillow of curb, tan parka tucked

under her chin, surrounded

by what were mother, brother, family friend,

their dead legs splayed like broken chairs,

and out of photo range, we're told,

a small dog in green carrying case, barking.

Tell me, how do I keep from falling apart?

*

When I was her age and couldn't sleep,
I tossed my bedclothes on the floor,
pretended my parents died of cholera
in India, just like in *A Little Princess*
or *The Secret Garden*.

Now, I was an orphan. I had to lie at night
        in a room with invisible others,
        our beds bare mattresses
            (for effect, I tossed the bedclothes off)

and imagined
        a wealthy couple, say,
        in oil-rich Texas, looking for a little girl.

They sent presents, from America!
        First a floaty white sheet I could drape
        over my 48-pound frame.

Next, a blanket.
        It was so warm.
        Last, the pillow

cool from the linoleum floor.
        It always made me drowsy.

*

On the ground behind Alisa's body

a blue roller suitcase; inside a girl's

pink tank top, pants, and pairs

of blue and yellow socks.

*

I remember the tender face of your youngest

grandchild in your phone, and the long legs

of red anemones and iris you tended

back home. And the autumn

you wrote about the symphony,

the hall quite full, and everyone

brought gas masks. *It was Brahms,*

you wrote, *Fantastic*!

I remember your eyes, always full of love and sorrow.

*

Now another girl-- blond wisps

and almond eyes—begins to sing

in the bomb shelter, in Ukrainian,

in her mind, she's Elsa, in *Frozen,*

serenading the sallow people as they rest

on towels and piles of clothes,

whatever they could grab as they ran.

.

Ta kholodu, she sings,

let winter come,

ya ne lvaka vusyo

I'm not afraid of the cold.

Brava, Amelia, they clap and clap

while here we hit replay and watch her

over and over. We want to launch

a rain of blue and yellow winning tickets

over her, we want to pluck her up

and help her fly away

When I was her age I would clap and clap

to rescue Tinkerbell and chant *I do I do*

believe in fairies I do I do

*

Meanwhile today's headline:

Ukraine Fatigue Surfaces in U.S. Poll

as we complain about gas prices

and buy an extra lottery ticket

and 48 rolls of toilet paper

and figurines from *Frozen* made in China

and ice cream

and whisper silently

not me not me not me

America

sometimes I want to spit you out of my mouth

*

O my friend, whose gun is hidden

on the roof, who knows decades

of gas masks and rockets –

teach me to listen to the rain.

The last time we met

you peeled a mango in the sun

and slipped it slice by slice

to me. Help me.

I need to remember that sweetness.

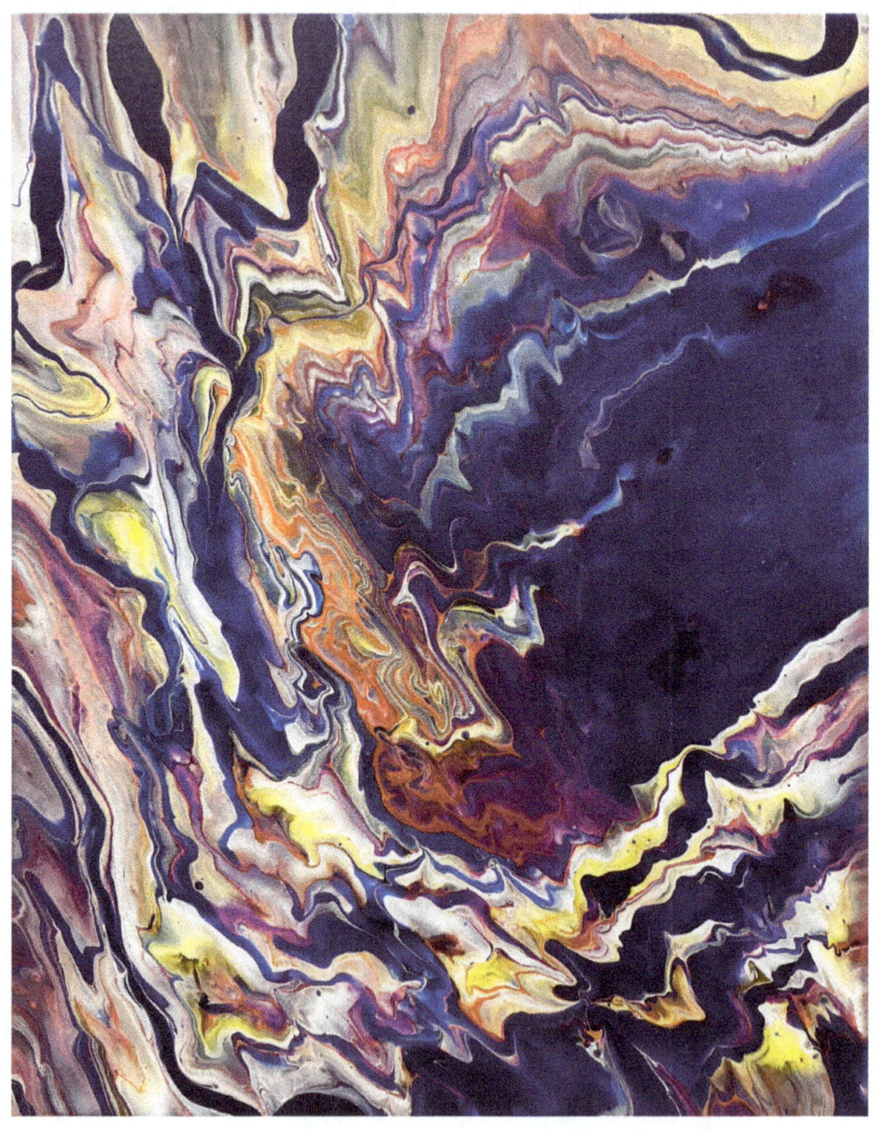

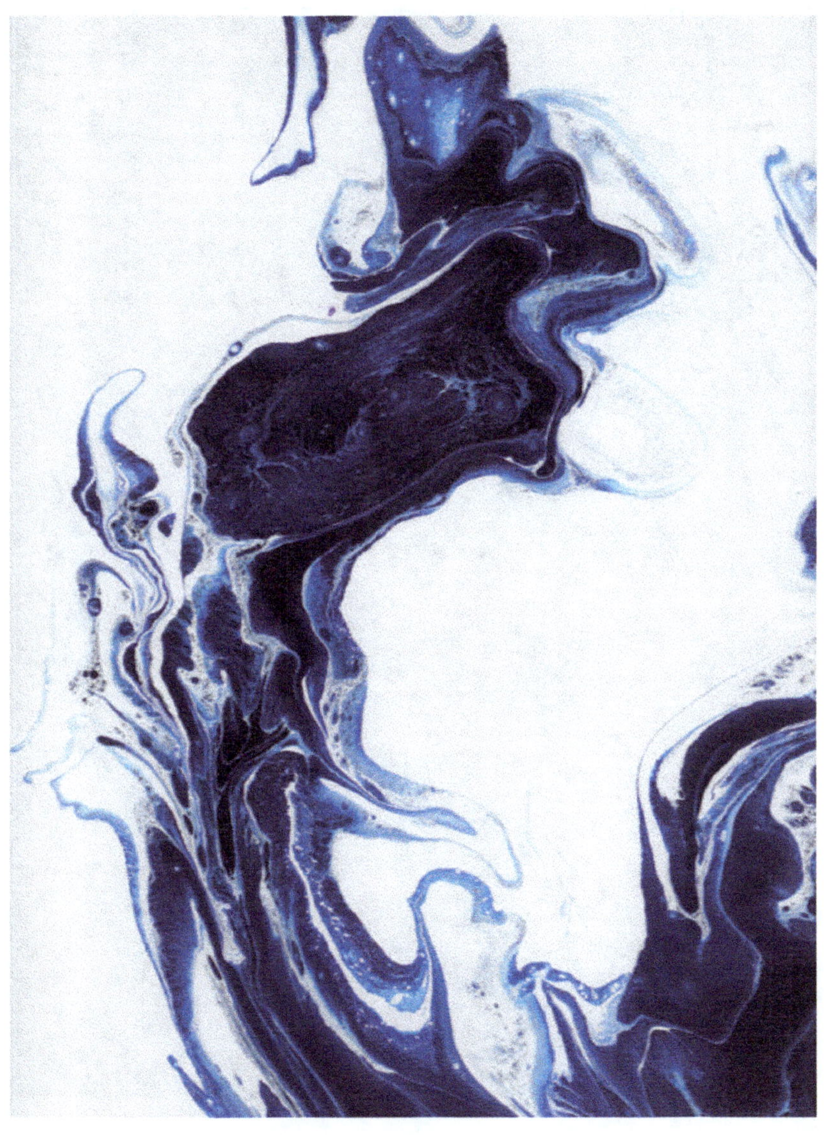

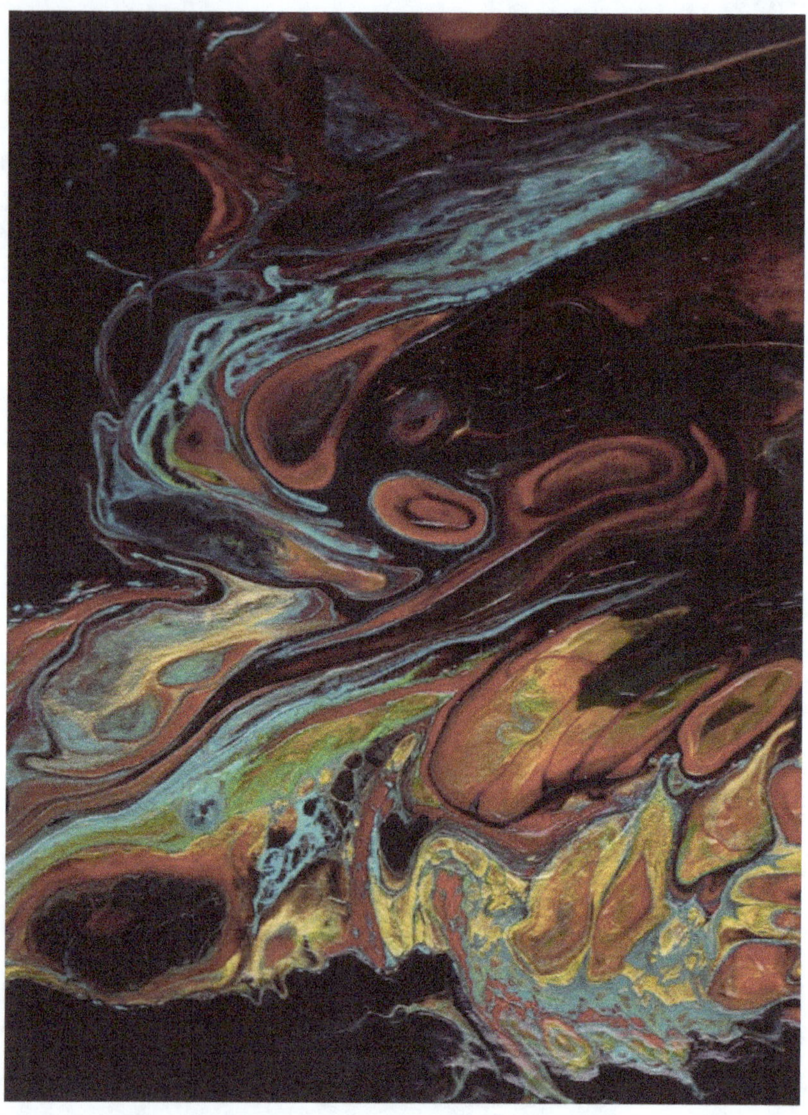

Memoria

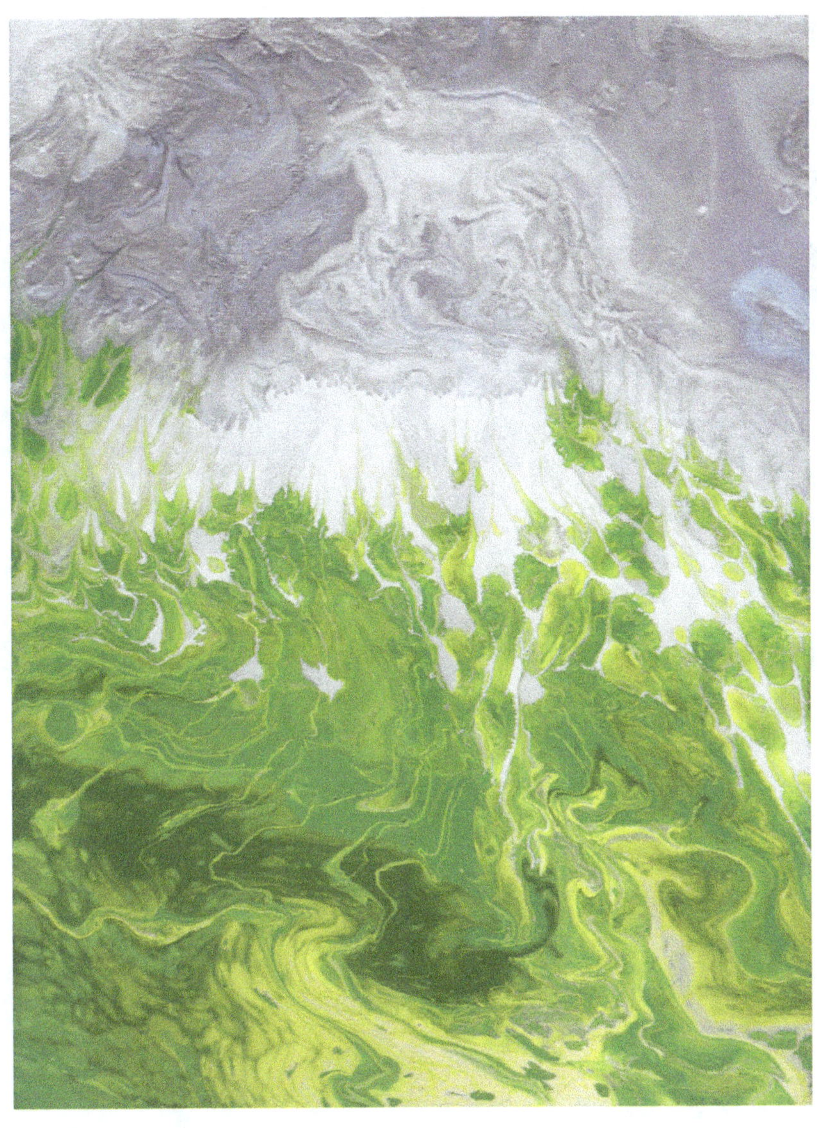

EMILY RANKIN

Opuntia

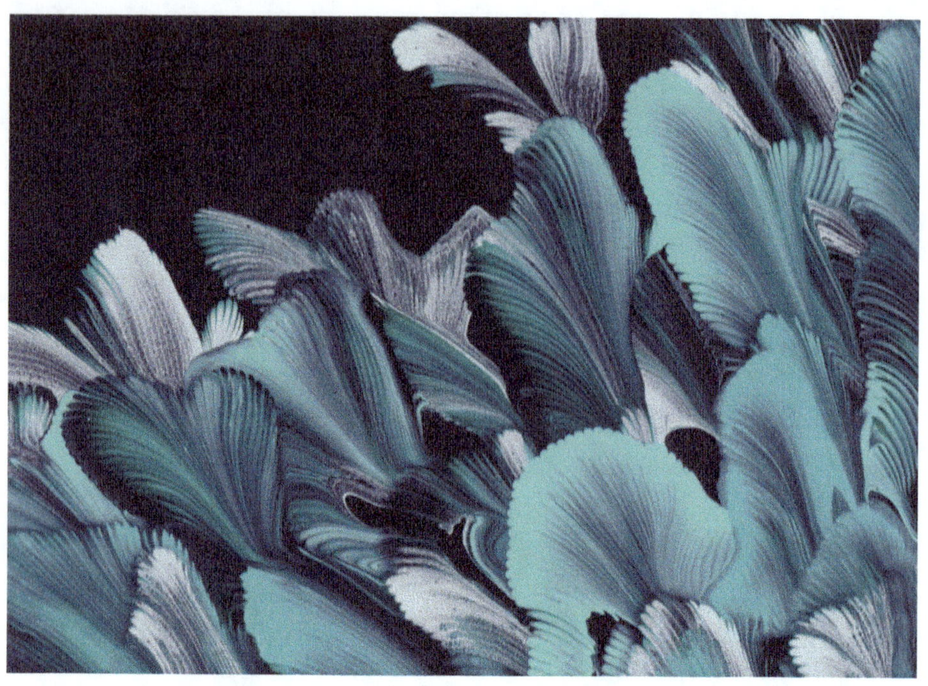

                                        River

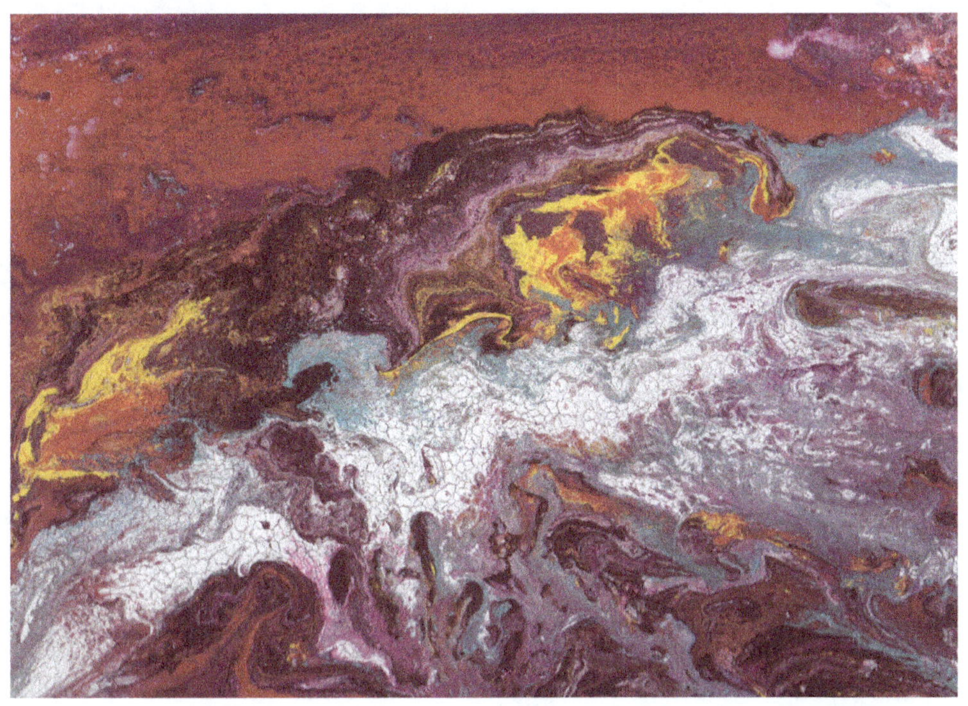

FRANK PAINO

Terracotta Army

> *The figures in Emperor Qin Shi Huandgi's famous terracotta army
> were painted with brilliant realism; however, within four minutes
> of being exposed to air, the pigments fade completely.*

After more than two millennia,

a stone visage crowns

beneath a farmer's hand.

Soon, a long sleep will begin

to shatter as eight-thousand

terracotta men in armor,

horses, acrobats, bronze cranes

and lazing swans are raised

from their lullaby of earth,

quicksilver, and burnt timber.

But for now, it's just this

guileless man who regards

a long-ago face, fractured

but rendered brilliant

through alchemies of iron

oxide, azurite, and cinnabar

that conjure the breathless

artifice of life,

though only for the time

it takes to wonder

at such wild proficiency

before the color flakes

like scales that spangle

a seine net,

the fragment going dun

as a dried gourd, its hues

not bled but vanished,

like the dream of immortality.

FRANK PAINO

Still

"It is her one work, and it is not easy."
                    — Gayle Boss ("A Turtle's Silver Bead of Quietude")

Late October, and the painted turtle
who, summer days, staked her claim
on the upthrust fist of an old pier piling,
lifts her head for a final measure of sun,
of breath, before she drops her body's
plated anchor into the cooling lake.

Down now, past jade combs of eelgrass
and milfoil, snarls of hornwort and fishing line,
to a place where the full-moon countenances
of lily pads purl their roots.

There, she hollows the soft tomb
in which she'll lie 'til spring,
armored scutes like amulets with no light
to set them burning, while Canadian winds
dive into Ohio's northern counties,
seal this small lake with a pall
of tarnished ice.

Eyes sealed, limbs drawn into their cage
of keratin and bone, she'll go still as a saint
who contemplates heaven's lanterned footpaths,
her heart, too, gone quiet as the tongue of a bell,
untolled, her life hinged on that last in-breath

while lactic acid pours its poisoned spell
into her veins and her body begins to surrender
its only antidote, leeching calcium
from shell and bone until she begins to soften,
the weight of water growing in equal measure
to her piecemeal vanishing,
the cure nearly worse than the curse,

and nothing to sustain her
but this fraught tranquility
that will vouchsafe the numbered days
lengthening toward April's green's ubiquity,
that fist of softened pine which will hold her,
once again, in summer's scintillant thrall.

WENDY DREXLER

Two Dead Dolphins, Blackfish Creek, Wellfleet

An acrid stench laced with ammonia,
    steeped in slow rot
        and the uncorseting of flesh.

Gutted and swollen. Stranded at low tide,
    they must have gasped for air.

    My son and daughter-in law, their baby boy
snuggled in a pack on her chest, don't want to look,
    walk quickly past.

    I draw close—not sure if it's mere
fascination, to see exactly what death makes of us,

or to honor the delicate veins that mapped the flukes,
    their aerodynamic arch, their once-ease
    and power finessing the water,

and the great corsage of the intestines, spilled out,
    light brown worms swarming
    the seeping organs,

and the architecture—the gently arching nave
    of ribs that buttressed the flesh,

the orb of the now-empty eye socket,
    the long tapering snout,
        and the slightly open jaw
with its almost doll-like,
    evenly spaced rows of teeth—

and I look for a long time, and consider touching,
    but do not, the forehead's
        swell of melon
    that looks as soft and vulnerable
as the fontanelles on a baby's head.

WENDY DREXLER

Cecropia Moths

What are their lives for, their first ten months
encased in cocoon, molting through four instars,
wintering like dried leaves
on thin branches or the trunks of black cherry trees
to emerge with a seven-inch wingspan
and a fifty-fifty chance
of being eaten by a bird, their only protection,
camouflage—the black owlish eyespots,
the leathery grey, black, and beige wingtips
scarily resembling the side of a snake's head—
these moths that live a scant five days
without guts or a mouth, eating nothing,
the male navigating by moonlight,
pheromones, and feathery antennae to find
a female a mile away, and the female
driven to lay one hundred eggs before she dies—
lives built for survival, not for beauty.
Maybe I find them beautiful because I, too,
have been made for survival, gestating
in the long slow cocoon of childhood,
and I, too, have practiced the beauty of deception.
As when, at twelve or thirteen, fearing I would be
easily spotted, I padded my bra with Kleenex
anyway, testing my wings with spin the bottle
in Janet Milstein's dark basement, hormone-driven,
later camouflaged in high heels, miniskirts,
my eyelashes curled, my lips painted sometimes
Raven Red, sometimes Cherries in the Snow.

WENDY DREXLER

For My Neighbor Who's Lived Across the Street from Me for Twenty-four Years

After months of not seeing you, I almost don't
recognize you out on your driveway as one
of the several younger men who live with you

wheels you to a waiting car. How brittle, thin,
and stiff you are, like a doll, as he lifts you
from the chair and carries you to the open door,

folds you down into the seat. Years ago, when you
were still walking with a cane, you'd told me you'd
been in remission from MS for years, that symptoms

had returned. Now your skin has a sheen, as if your
insides were spinning a cocoon, consuming you.
I debate saying hello, prod myself to walk over.

Say something inane, like *Nice to see you again.*
How language fails us. *I haven't seen you in a while,*
wanted to come over and say hello (good-bye,

good-bye). *It looks like you're not doing so well*
(how inept!). Staring straight ahead, you don't turn
to look at me (maybe you can't). Maybe your eyes

swivel a little. Your cheeks, hollowed out, your body
as light as the newspaper you once wrote for.
This tyrant disease, converting you to bone. But then

I see how this muscular younger man who'd carried
you in his arms to the car, after he'd settled you into
the seat, leaned over and kissed your cheek, softly,

tenderly. Whether lover or friend, caregiver, muse,
or nurse. Am I not, in a poem, supposed to tell you
I cried? And said something stupid again, there at the end,

It looks like you're getting good care. Did you nod?
Bob, I hope that kiss soothed your tractionless muscles,
your attenuated nerves. I hope that kiss was song.

RUTH C. CHAD

Ancient Song

Shtetl   steerage

     shock

symphony

     of tongues

my ancestors' lyrics

covering   my nakedness

on the edge

     of knowing

where is the moon in fog?

ANDY HOFFMAN

Liberty Leading

I met Eugene Delacroix once over lunch
 in my high-school cafeteria.

We spoke in French, which surprised me,
 as I don't speak French.

I did not recognize him until he conjured
 in the air 'Liberty Leading the People.'

:I hate that people know this, he said :but not me!
 "But it lives," I told him, "and you're dead."

:I suppose, he answered :but I'd rather
 switch positions. Wouldn't you?

He said :Most artists apply perfection
 only to the art of the boring.

:Draw from the violent dictionary of nature!
 I wish I could paint that violently.

:The great artists stole, but they knew what to steal,
 whereas the lesser one just take gilt flowers.

I took notes. :Scholars can only find
 what's already there. Artists discover invisible bonds.

:If you want to be an artist, he told me,
 build a bridge to another soul.

We talked for an hour. When he left, I found
 myself sitting just as I had when he arrived.

People tell me, "You just imagined him!"
 :No, I've explained ever since. :He imagined me

CAROLYN OLIVER

Westering

Dear B———

               I do not know

if this season can be a friend

to you. The rain has stopped

insisting; soon every tree turns

inward. Mornings I think of you:

your hair, silver-rippling;

your voice, an evening lioness

at rest on still-warm earth;

your far-ness, sunrise yet to seek

you, westering. No easy harbor.

But it is with your humility,

your adamance, that cove pines

endure the salt wind's chisel,

and baywater laughs your laugh,

loping to embrace the rocks.

KAREN EARLE

I Would Hold You Gently

you snow   you shroud

you trapdoor   you cloud

you hammer   you screech

you high heat   you certain

cold bones   you river

grumbler-to-the-sea

blush you   branch

sprout   you mumbler

penitent   ice-edged   lips

sequestered   you spring

swollen   rock golden

you wind grifter

you river   of knives

slender taper

burning   black iris

flame-sharp   you dog

star-scorched   you gaggle

you rain-swollen river

rain-bowed berries

quiver of light

you repaired   you silence

stick   knife   gun

you cicada-scream

o sweet skulls

you

DONNA SPRUIJT-METZ

Engine

I sit

at day's stilled rudder,

the splayed light

settling over the milkweed

—weightless crowns—here

I am—in the thicket—YOU

always so far   ahead of me—

not quite out of sight—and here

is my heart—pointing

towards the man I have loved

for so long—I have forgotten

how not to love him—I place my hand

on his chest.   —every morning—

for strength—to withstand the rising

from our bed—to face the Engine

again—

LEILA FARJAMI

Finding You

I lost you in the crowd.

Years bulged like dead sparrows,

motionless, grey.

I scoured the sky.

You were not there.

At thirteen,

slumped, waiting for the school bus,

you spoke one language: *Immigrant.*

In the wintery gust, your legs shivered,

eyes, welled up.

You sat in the classroom, didn't say or get a word,

slipped out, sobbed the entire 10 a.m. recess.

No blade in the shower, you saved yourself.

What began to gnaw you inside was anorexia

—belly hollowed out to hold the corpse

of all swallowed pain—

your first boyfriend cheated,

the ache stabbed you

limb to limb.

No sun, you grew phantom bones,

a holed heart—

embarked on a pilgrimage

to grief—

a god with no temple.

***

I remember your favorite verse of Rumi:
The wound is where the light enters,

your fingers crawling

under the earth like fish burrowing in mud,

searching for signs of life beneath all frozenness,

a body,

thawing,

easing toward

its own fire.

SHANNON K. WINSTON

Blueprints

For Anna Atkins (1799-1871) who is often considered the first female photographer.

Anna waded into the sea when it was so fresh and pure and purely fresh,

     when the light hit the water like a knife. She collected specimens in silver

buckets to examine with her father. Oh, to work side by side with a famous

     zoologist, chemist, and mineralogist who extracted silver from ore.

I envy her: the way her father taught her to use a microscope, to catalogue plants

     by their scientific names, to classify animals according to geography and species.

I want that: for my father, an architect, to teach me about right angles,

     compasses, and fine-tip pens. I want to dig an Exacto knife

through cardboard, make triangles, rectangles, and squares that, in turn,

     build walls, roofs, gutters. How precise and fine-tuned are the model homes

with paper bushes, green paper lawns, and blue-glue rivers that run alongside borders.

     All of it small enough to carry: all of it scaled, a hypothetical of *what*

could be—not yet *what might have been*; the implementation is harder,

     which is maybe why my father rolled his blueprints into a dusty corner

of the garage and said: *I'm done.* And maybe this is why he came into my life like a wave,

     intermittently. His waves were tired, slumpy. They sagged their shoulders as if the mere thought of curling their salty hurl was too much.

    In and out, out and in, out, out, out—out to sadness and grief.

Sometimes, I Google my father. On Zillow, I find his old apartment remodeled

    by a developer and take a virtual tour. Room by room, I identify vestiges:

a door, a spiral staircase, a green stone fireplace. I'm tracing a face.

    Would I recognize my father on the street? Some days, I pretend he might

have stayed if he had been a famous zoologist, chemist, and mineralogist.

    I imagine Anna collecting algae, birds overhead.

She places Irish moss and kelp between paper and glass. I hover over her shoulder.

    When she's not looking, I snatch a blueprint and slip it

into my pocket. Negatives, positives, blue, blue—

    I'm a collector, a robber, a co-opter of other women's fathers.

SHANNON K. WINSTON

View from the Window at Le Gras

> —For Joseph Nicéphore Niépce *who is credited with taking the*
> *first photograph circa 1827. This poem borrows its title from the*
> *name of his photograph.*

Tell me about the pear tree, the barn's slanted roof,

and the bakehouse behind it. Let me smell the sourdough rise

in the early morning. Let me feel the loaf's ridges as I rip

off a corner and shove warm, soft grains into my mouth.

Tell me about the lavender oil you used as a solvent

and the bitumen of Judea, which is thick as tar

and affixes the light just so. When did you know

these ingredients would make your images stick?

Teach me your recipe. I, too, yearn for permanence.

Read me the letter you sent to your sister before

any of this worked, when you produced only negatives.

Her encouragement made it all possible, or so I'd like to think.

An amateur artist, at first you traced what you saw:

a horse, a man. A man trying to tame a petulant horse.

The print: ink on stubborn paper. Everything begins with a sketch.

Walk me through the way you slipped a plate into your camera obscura and stood at your window to take the first photograph.

Show me where you stood in your bedroom. Point out

your oval-shaped table lamp, the slippers to the right of your bed.

Let me touch your wrinkled sheets that caught shadows in their folds.

The hours unfolded and slowly the scene emerged:

a slanted roof, a pear tree, a bakehouse.

Only it's blurred and dented on a pewter plate.

I squint and barely make out a triangle and thick mottled walls

of distant buildings. Teach me how to angle the aperture

and the pinhole, how to avoid overexposure. Show me

what you might have done differently if you could do it again.

Before us, fine lines rise like yeast, like sweet crumbs on the tongue.

SHANNON K. WINSTON

The Autochrome

Before a young woman in red silks kneels on a rocky beach,[1]

before a woman in a puffy blue dress and pink coat sits and knits

in an archway in the Netherlands,[2] and before a girl pets

the white rabbit nestled in her coral dress,[3]

came the farmers who planted the potatoes that made

the starch that made color possible in the first place.

Six-inch holes in the earth, calloused hands, hunched backs,

a purple September chill. I'm Louis Lumière. Lumière,

meaning light. In my studio in Lyon, I pass

potato grains—only a thousandth of a millimeter—through sieves.

Red-orange, blue, and green dyes dapple the color filter:

a piece of glass onto which I add layer after layer

with a make-up brush and a press. I add the emulsion.

Silver halide bites my skin. Let's call it anticipation. Eager hands

will snatch these plates, slip them into cameras, and watch the world blush.

1 Autochrome by Mervyn O'Gorman.
2 Autochrome by Wilhelm Tobien.
3 Autochrome by Thomas Shields Clark.

But that will come later. Later, when the potato starch will soak up

pinkish hues, violet blues, the human eye will flesh

out the rest. And even later, the glass plates will seem muted

and imprecise: the woman in red silks on a rocky beach

will be long gone. The knitter, the rabbit, and coral dress, too.

What's a synonym for loneliness?

My plates will be stored in tight black boxes

to shield them from the light. But that will be much later.

Now, the sunlight speckles my studio window.

Elsewhere, three harvesters cut and bind wheat.[4]

And as the woman in a pale gray dress gathers her sheaves,

she mutters about the light over the fields, how it goes on forever.

[4] Autochrome by Hans Hildenbrand.

JESSICA GOODFELLOW

The Patron Saint of Remembering is Also the Patron Saint of Forgetting

My father was forbidden to ride the ponies,

aged nine years old, another motherless summer in New Mexico.

He's forgotten my sisters, my children, me, but this he remembers,

a story I've never heard before. He repeats it four times in one day.

Only childhood remains for him, a powerless time—it's strange.

Why not recall the triumphs of his career—the big contract with Edison,

or the congregation's admiration after his Sunday lessons on repentance?

Where are the memories of car trips to the Badlands and Rush-

more? Why live in the memory of insignificance and rage? This is what I was

thinking while I lay listening to the distant storm, curled like a fetus, ever

unimagined by my father, an unspooled nothingness.

Unimagined by my father, unspooled into nothingness. . .

thinking while I lay listening to the distant storm, curled like a fetus. Ever-

more, why live in the memory of insignificance and rage? This is what I was.

Where are the memories of car trips to the Badlands, and the rush

of the congregation's admiration after his Sunday lessons on repentance?

Why not recall the triumphs of his career, the big contract with Edison?

Only childhood remains; for him, a powerless time. It's strange—

a story I've never heard before—he repeats it four times in one day.

He's forgotten my sisters, my children, me, but this he remembers—

aged nine years old, another motherless summer in New Mexico,

my father was forbidden to ride the ponies.

JOCELYN DOWNEY ROYALTY

Things There Are

There is a house in the city.
Something like a haunting.

There is a rolling blackout. A smattering
of stars. We are failing to see this place
in all its beauty, says my father, while we
are sitting on the fire escape
pretending to remember.

There is a raccoon who has taken up residence
in our compost bin. There are baby racoons
following her everywhere, cooing something silky
into the endless heat.

There is a Scrabble board. My mother
crying in the kitchen. I promise
I'll be better.

I keep coming home
& saying it's the last time.
I talk to the pigeons on the sill, growing fat
with white bread. Tell me
how to fill with water. Tell me
how to make an ultimatum and keep it.

There is a cordless hairdryer. There is a local election on.
There is my father, his face screwed into the faint
and glowing anger of a child.
There is a picture of my grandmother, age five,
dancing in her underwear in her front lawn.
He's put photos of her
next to my school pictures, as if to point
to her eyes. How they screw the same
mixed-up smile as mine. As if to say that we
are two incarnations of the same angry ball of light.

There is a plastic surgeon in Belfast, the father
of an old boyfriend, who says he can remove
my grandmother's face from mine. I bring him pictures
of her, and he shows me where he could edit:
my soft browbone, the bump in my nose. My driftwood
mouth. I ask him if he can change other things. The register of my voice.
My height. The pearl of sadness that has been growing in my throat
since I was a little girl. I ask him if he has seen
SpyKids. I ask him if he could retrofit me like Carmen Cortez,
so I could shoot bullets out my wrists, or press a button
on the back of my neck
and call up a forcefield,
and he says okay,
but let's start with the basics.

There is a house in the city. There is a part of me
intent on forgiving.

There is a folk tale I remember only half of. A crow
wants the water at the base of a clay jug, and spends the day
filling it with rocks & that is all I have:
half story, pottery
all choked up with stone.

JOCELYN DOWNEY ROYALTY

Sestina with Five Definitions

Adolfo Quimbamba: An Angolan basketball player, now retired
Quimbambas: The boonies
Chimbomba: a balloon
Las quimbambas: Often defined as donde Cristo perdió el gorro
Quimbamba: The nothingness/the distance

The bloodhound follows you everywhere.

To the corner store, where you fill your bags with cumquats and white rice,

to the silver plaque commemorating your father on the highway island

where you kneel and get sand in your jeans, leave a trading card with the face of

Adolfo   Quimbamba

smiling back up at you. Miles South, a siren cries out from the brushfire

and the bloodhound looks past you, resists the guttural bolt that comes with being canine.

She is nothing if not canine.

The mountain goats, not as prey as they look, scaffold the mountainside everywhere

from this side of the Sonoran to the West End condos engulfed in brushfire.

You watch the summer sculpt a ghost of where the water used to be, depressions like rice

thumbed by a spoon. You and your dog live out here, in the quimbambas

because you like how big the sky gets at night. You think that this could be an island

if you closed your eyes. Yes — this place could be an island

with only dust and the blue of morning reflecting in your canines

when you look horizon. This place a magic 8-ball, blown up like a chimbomba

while the Philco statics in the living room. You think about where

you must have left your keys. The bloodhound follows you to your car, nudges you, smelling of rice

from that Korean place in Tucson, the one where you served bibimbop for months, 'till you got fired.

You: unemployed, un-island, un-fathered with your hands on the steering wheel, scallions and fire

still in the fabric of your hoodie. Your phone links to the Bluetooth of your car without asking. I land

at noon, says a voicemail. I'll be by the pretzel stand. The bloodhound whines, and you shred like jackfruit, rice

pouring out from you like someone pierced your bag with a paring knife. The dog's kind and empty canine

looking up at you from the passenger seat. You tell her how you see your father everywhere:

glaring in the black eyes of frogs, in the cauterized hearts of hollow cacti, mirage'd in the quimbambas.

The bloodhound follows you following your father into the quimbambas.

Out here, says a memory, is where Jesus lost his cap. Something holy burned in bushfire.

All summer long, the dog has watched you complain about Jesus. All summer, boys in cars whistled whore

while you waited for the bus in your tank top. All summer long, afternoon sweat itself into an island.

The bloodhound howls, really howls, like you've never heard before. In another life, she could've been a K9

recruit, sniffing the bleached ground for a cadaver. She waits for you in the morning, to sniff the rice

you cook in the crockpot. Good, Christian rice. Rice white with death, peppered with okra, the kind of rice

that could inflate with every memory of your father cheering for Angola as Quimbamba

ballets the end-line. You want some wine, some simple canine

mercy in the moonlight. The horizon fills with fire, and here you are a good daughter. Only fire

creeping softly to the borders of your bedroom, the threshold that makes you an island.

Turn off the 9 o'clock news. You're a good daughter. She's a good dog. There's warmth everywhere, everywhere

your father's crackled voice tells you to meet him at the pretzel stand. Fire-

light through the last luminaria left over from Christmas twinkles in the quimbamba.

Dad, you say into the phone. You wish it could be that easy. His voice long gone, and so everywhere.

JOCELYN DOWNEY ROYALTY

More than ever

Scientists are spotting black bears on the Eastern Seaboard.
Dan took me to the place
he saw one last. We sat in the back yard of a friend of a friend
and waited for miracles. Tell me about your father, he said. He was
being nice, but I told him anyway. My room of echoes
in my childhood home. Bathwater and a bruise. Nothing
more than that. How I wrote my journal entries

in the margins of cookbooks, where no one would never think
to find them. Dan makes his face
burn with sympathy. In a few hours, a bear will creep out
from the old growth, and come close to the screen porch. It will be
so close that its fur will impress on the mesh
the way our housecat leans her body against the window
to feel the breeze. But we will not be here then. We will not

see the gentle shape of her, this animal, this massive
malnourished thing rifling through the garbage bins, looking
for something fragrant. We will not be there to wonder
whether she has babies, the way you're meant to wonder
when you see a bear. By then, Dan and I

will be in his car, almost to the diner
while he flicks cigarette butts into the hot mouth of summer.
I'll put on a song that goes, I'm afraid
that I need men. Isn't that a little on the nose?
He'll ask. The treeline golden in the setting sun
like a postcard. Twilight glinting with the eyes
of prey animals. Do you think
we'll ever see it? I'll ask, talking
about the bear, and he'll hear it
all wrong, like I'm referring
instead to angels, and he'll say,
maybe someday.

MICHAEL MORETH

Acceptable

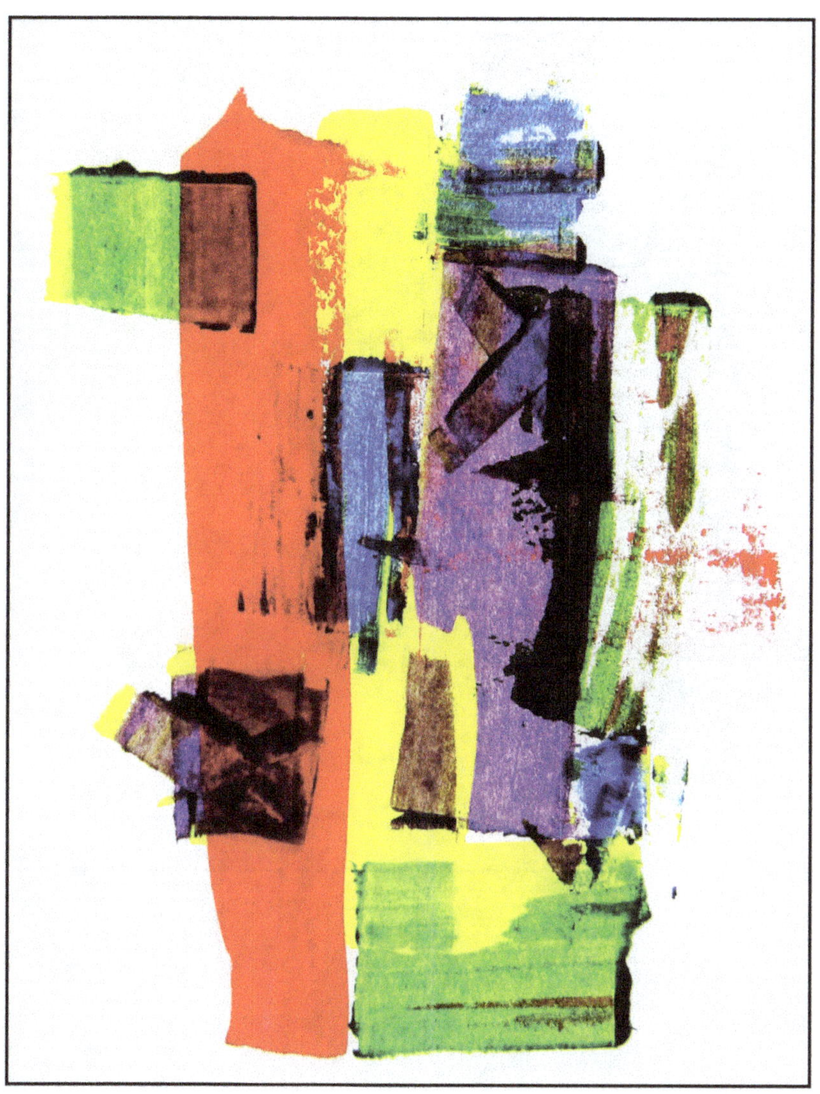

MICHAEL MORETH   **Yare**

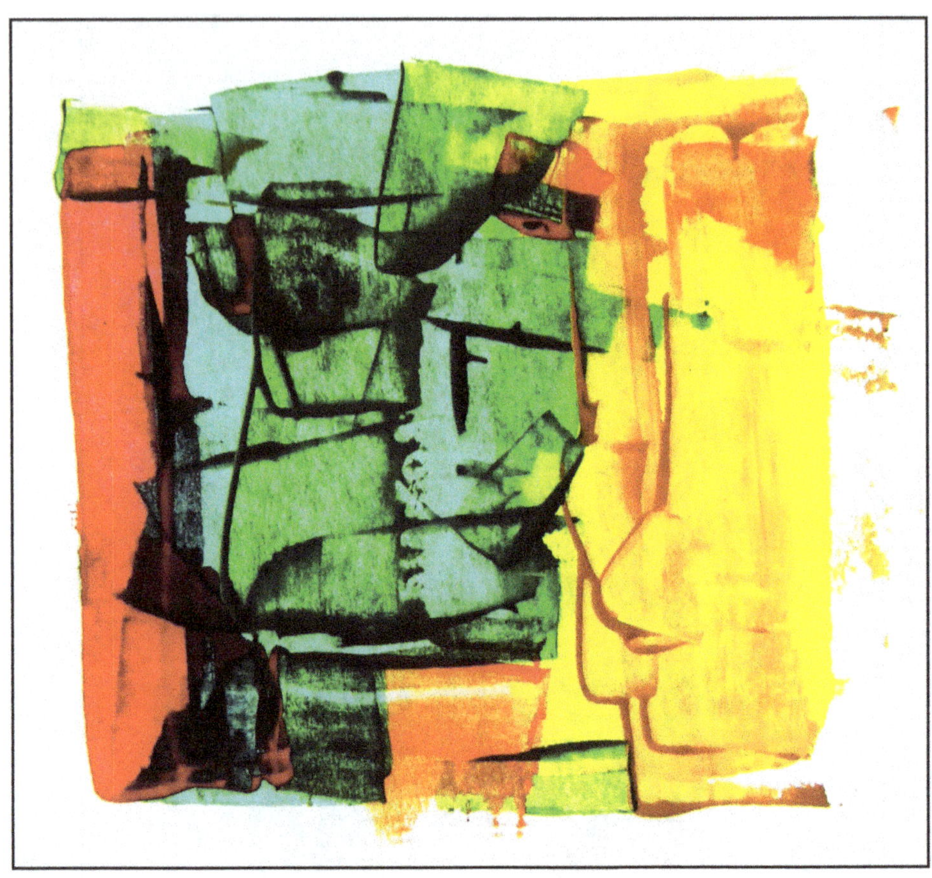

MICHAEL MORETH **Zealed**

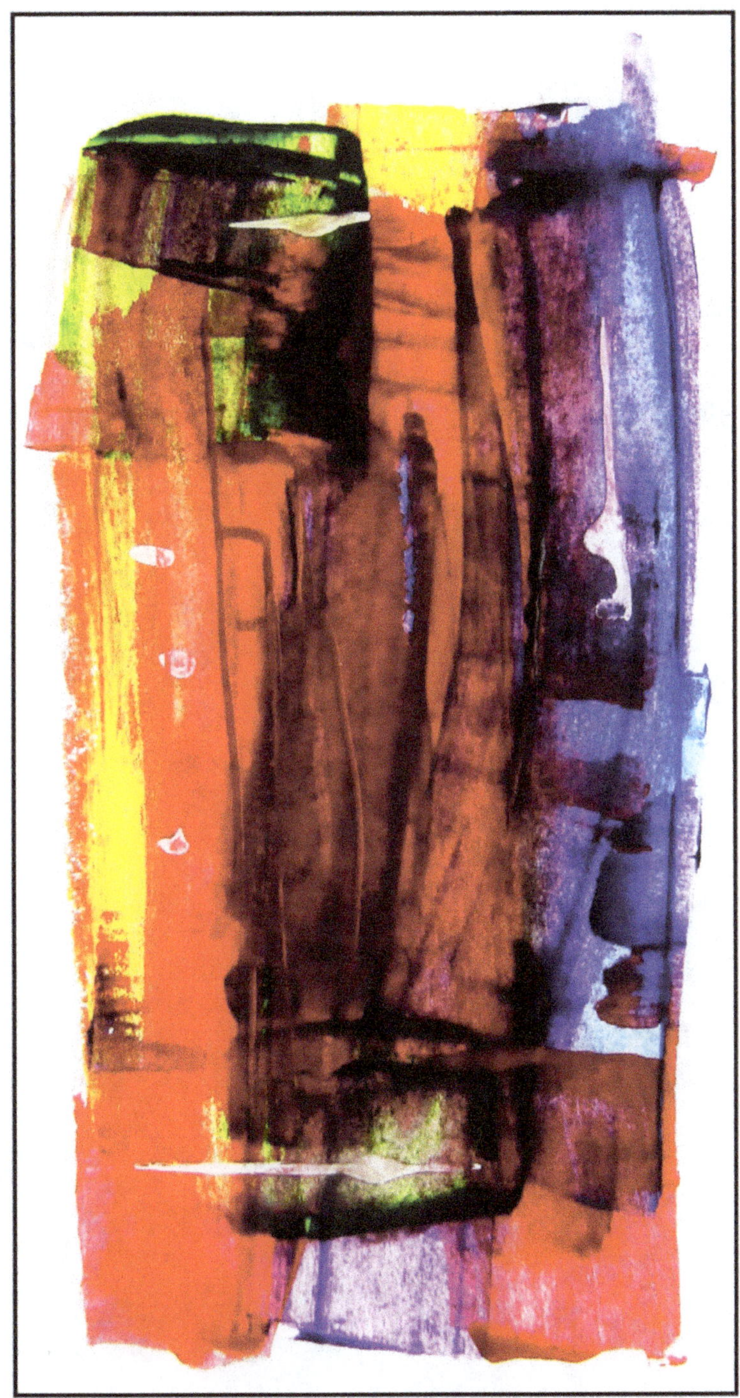

KAREEM TAYYAR

In Elementary School

you did not dream
of being an astronaut,

but of being the moon
in the years before

the astronauts arrived,
when starlight shone like

a written language
with a thousand different

words for "love."

does this mean you were
always a romantic?

or does it mean that
you simply longed to be

somewhere other
than where you were?

the moon might know,
but she isn't speaking.

& your inner child probably knows,
but he isn't either.

KAREEM TAYYAR

Elizabeth Bishop

Is telling me about miracles.
It's just the two of us.
Outside the sprinklers have come on,
as they do each night at precisely 10 o'clock.
She pauses to ask when was the last time I prayed.
I tell her to go on with her story.
Later we stand on the balcony & wait for rain.
It's late October.
She says she never remembers her dreams.
I tell her I know the feeling.

KAREEM TAYYAR

Cloud Ghazal

there is a name for a country composed entirely of clouds.
my father knew it,
& he said he would tell it to me when the time was right.

I dream about walking across the clouds
more often than I dream of flying.
one of these days I'll figure out what this means.

& on the eighth day God asked the angels
to create the clouds in his absence.
or at least that is what my grandmother always believed.

as a boy it would sadden me when the clouds changed shape.
perhaps it had something to do with my fear of aging,
which has remained with me ever since.

yesterday the ghost of my father called long distance
to say there was something he had wanted to tell me,
but that he couldn't remember what it was.

Kareem, all these years of looking up
at the clouds & you still haven't learned
it isn't them that you are trying to outrun.

KAREEM TAYYAR

In the Middle of My Life

I dreamed of Joan of Arc
riding a brown horse across a summer field.

I prayed often,
three or four times a day,

usually to a saint
who is said to look out for travelers.

I didn't travel,
except through empty cities

where the street signs had all been removed,
& the cathedrals were covered in snow.

I rinsed dishes that sometimes
levitated above the sink,

little flying saucers
trying to make sense of how

they'd arrived in this particular place.

I wrote letters to the dead
that sometimes arrived anyway,

& that sometimes,
though less frequently,

meant I received letters in return.

Come back, one read.
Go on, said another.

I dug graves that I slept in.

I crossed rivers without getting wet.

& regarding that dream about Joan of Arc:

I don't know what it means either.

KAREEM TAYYAR

Video Game

the maiden exists in a castle
that you will never find.

you think you are a prince.

or you wish you were a prince.

even though the forest
that you were certain

you would enter
has not yet appeared.

there are rivers everywhere.

white jaguars slumber
upon the backs of dark clouds,

unsure of their roles.

each time a rain begins to fall
you long to enter a church.

sometimes you locate a church.

candles are lit.

the stories told by the stained glass
are ones you remember from earlier journeys when

vague apostles promised
a bounty of hidden maps.

maybe you still haven't survived
for as long as you need to.

& maybe this isn't the quest
you thought it would be.

not that it matters.

somewhere,
someone is waiting for your arrival.

you just hope they know
you're still on your way.

DMITRY BLIZNIUK

Sentenced Is Everyone

days of the week are extinct like dinosaurs

you won't find them anymore

instead you see

a gray bone or a tusk

or a rib as big as an oar

that used to belong to a Sundayceratops

war burns out time

curls its line

ties knots in it

and air alerts are a life sentence without parole

just turned inside out

and sentenced is everyone

a girl on a scooter

a soldier with a prosthetic arm

a woman walking a Rottweiler

DMITRY BLIZNIUK

Threadbare Leopards

it will take hundreds of years,
hundreds of years to determine the future.
I'm not there, I don't belong to that time.
fresh grass fills
last year's shell craters -
they look like threadbare leopards
in pale green sores.

JW SUMMERISLE

erebus

make your point with ineloquence;

i'm never sure
what to say. we

push off, pulling

boats behind us
on a sledge over

ice. it is piled

high with Bibles
and curtain poles.
domestic objects
we definitely

do not need.
but i can't
question it.

what is my place?

God, in absentia, sends
winds that strip us

thin and fill
our shoes with

sweat. frost

grows from
the body

and preserves. ice
can mummify. biting

wind can make a body
object.   i

consider singing
a song of Sir

Ranulph Fiennes, his
fingers in a drawer.

but it hasn't
come to that yet.

morale is high.

DANA MURPHY

Lilacism

After Aunt Adeline's WPA narrative, May 8, 1937

My mother used to
hide things.

A piece of cloth
had to be forgotten
to become
my pale blue dress.

Her hands didn't look like
they could spin wool
so quickly
when she wanted
to do something soft
and slow
for a while.

They stirred
vats of dye
so large
it defied
belief.

Her hard hands
cut steers into meat,
then sewed
brass buttons
by candlelight.

No one knew
of the small
batches of leaves
she picked carefully
in moonlit dew

until she taught me
the most delicate
"sort of lilac,"
the skin nestled
just under the hardest bark,
made colors
that did not yet
have names.

WENDY WISNER

After We Found Her

After we found her in the emergency room,
a thin white sheet draped over her body
as though to shield her nakedness from me—

after we decided she could no longer live alone
and we checked her into a hotel with my sister
until we figured it out—

after we hired a hazmat team to clean out her apartment:
four men dressed head-to-toe in shiny white protective gear,
their black gloved hands deep inside
my mother's kitchen sink—

I walked with her from the hotel to a café around the corner,
she leaning her heavy, warm body on mine,
and suddenly it began to snow: fierce, wild

chunks of snow whipping sideways past our faces,
and my mother—scared of rain and thunderstorms
and earthquakes and ice and snow

for her whole life—
began to laugh and laugh and laugh,
leaning the entire weight of her body against me now,
almost knocking me down.

CYNTHIA ATKINS

POEM WITH A BEAUTY PARLOR

When I call the front desk, the lady
at reception tells me that my mom
is having her hair done. At 92, she still wants
to look pretty—to feel good in her skin.
       Worth all the peroxides, and dyes,
and an olfactory salad of cosmetics.
In all their rooms, the typhoon of TV news
is telling of the disasters beyond the oxides
and lies. The body politic covering the gray old
       hairs and plinths of our judicial system.
In the palms of her hands, the beautician
is now holding my mother's small head.
So vulnerable to whatever gentle kindness
or evil her caregivers might dole out—
       I see all our fates held by mightier constructs.
Her fragile neck like a bird's. We used to know
the rule of law. I remember my young son asking
if my (divorced) parents had ever met? —
At 4, he'd never seen them in the same room.
I laughed; it was so funny. How could his innocence
understand they once shared a bedroom? —
       And from where I came.
America once shared a bedroom. My mother used
to own me to the grit and core of my being. I loathed
her for It. She *mother goosed* my brain with an unflinching
       aim at every weak spot. Older now, my mom
is getting more beautiful by the day, more mellow,
and I mean that—The poisons burned themselves out
like the sound a straw makes in a glass. She's grown glorious
petals— with the right apparatus, I think she could solve wars.

Ink on Paper

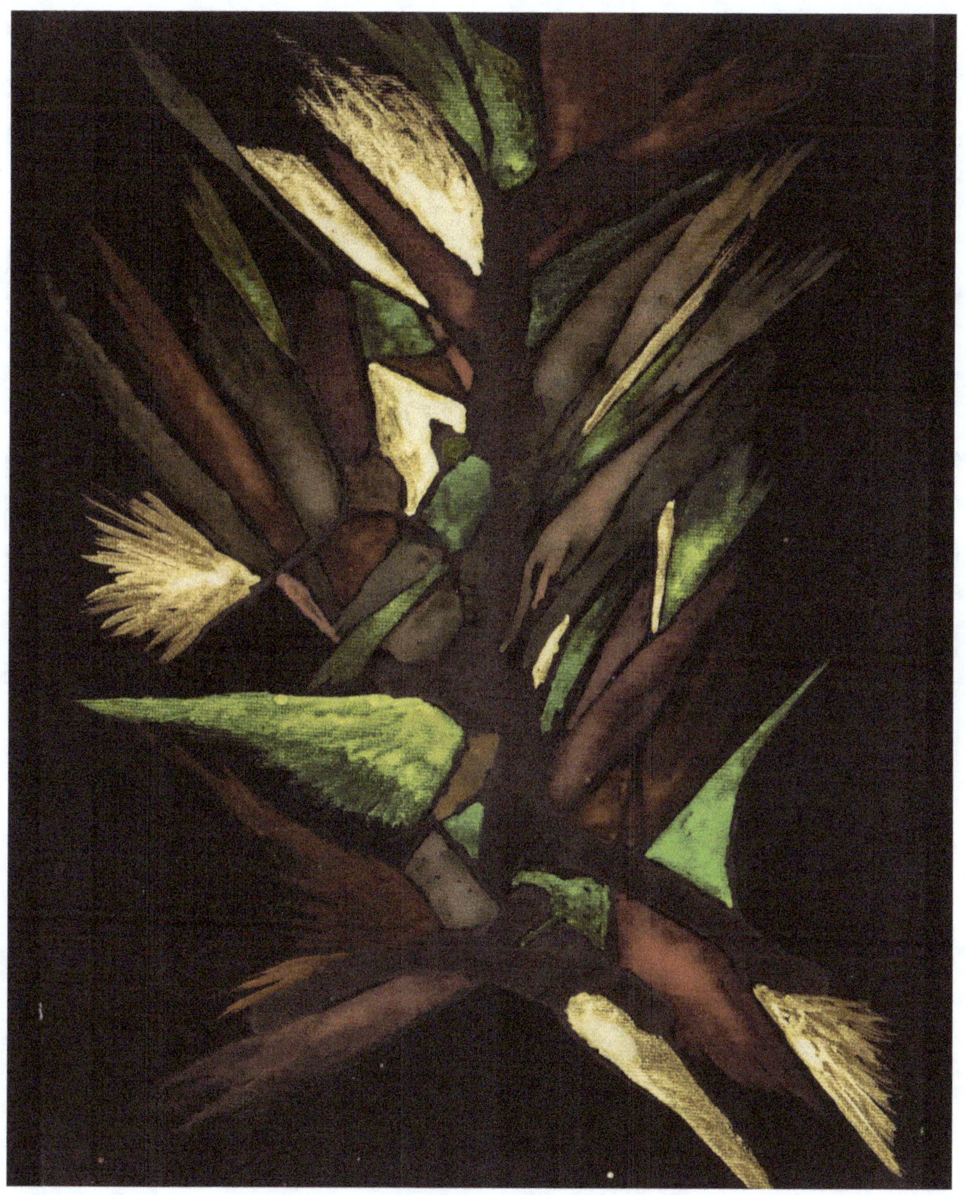

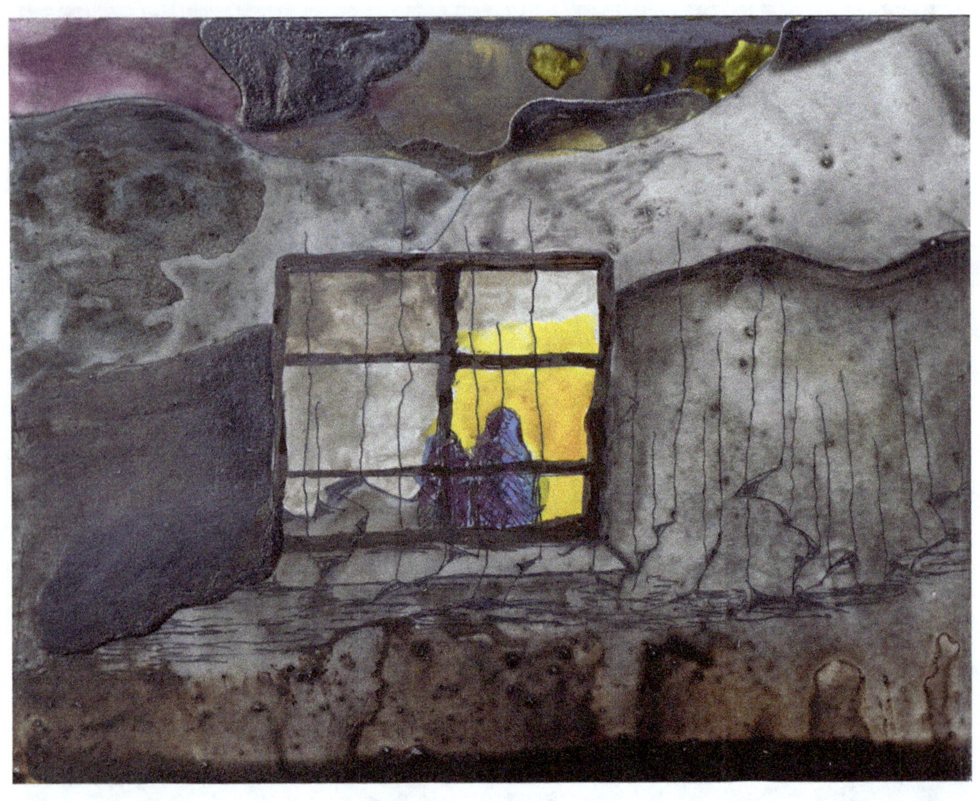

Cityscape

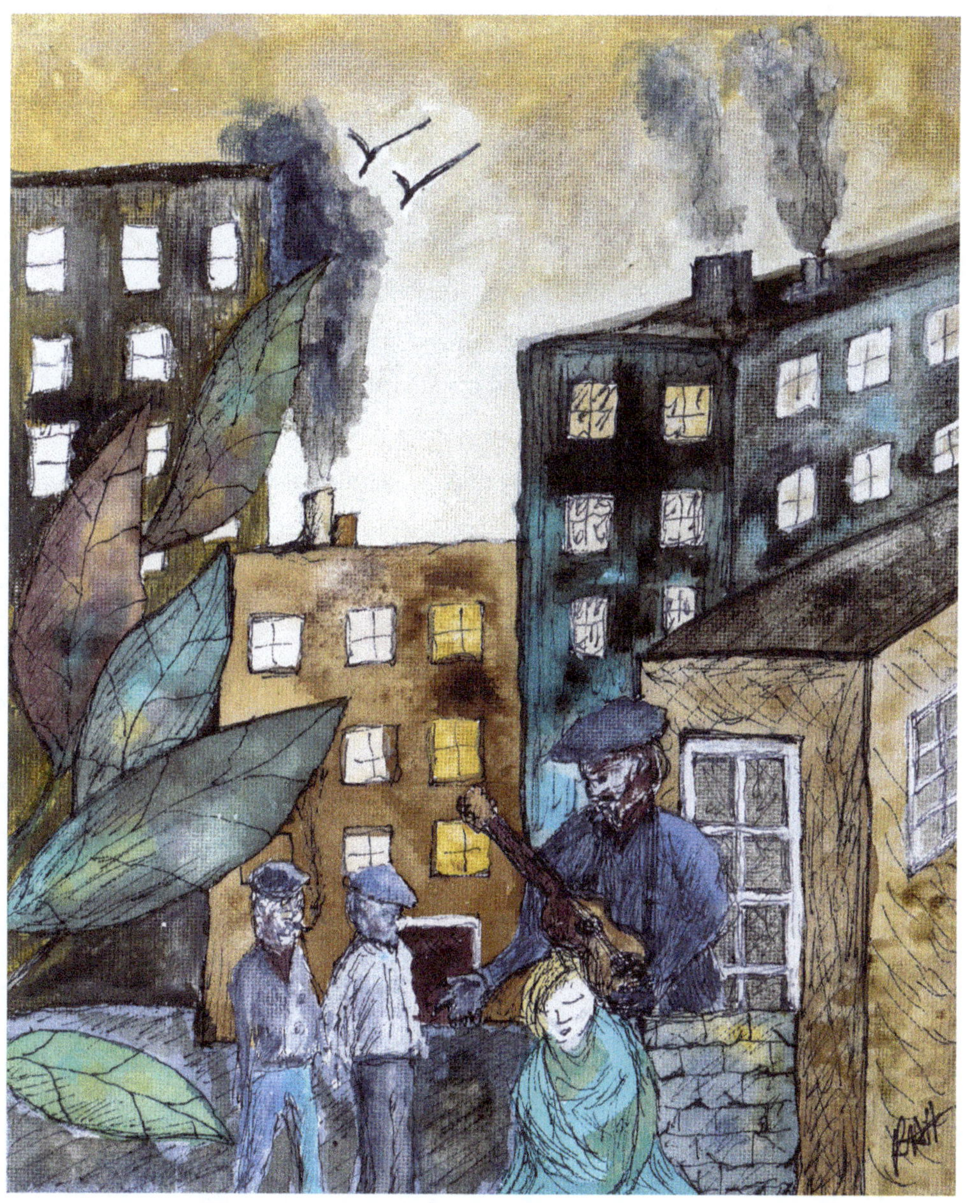

GABRIEL CLEVELAND

Evening Snow at Kanbara

after the woodblock painting by Utagawa Hiroshige, c. 1833-34

At last we lay eyes on Kanbara, quiet

in the moon's argent light. You look to me

and I see mountains of snow in your mind,

built up over our time on the cold roads.

Nothing but winter's white dust moves, wind-blown

like brush strokes on the canvas of this moment.

You turn West without another thought;

I watch the ground take the shape of your steps.

I know a bead of ice trails down your cheek

like it does on mine as I turn East.

In Spring, you'll sit and watch azaleas bloom;

paradise flycatchers will sing above.

I'll be a world or a dream away,

under a cherry tree North of Fuji.

MEGHAN STERLING

A Kinship with Emily D.

Again, the windows are bellowing
against the white curtains. Like gauze

over a wound, the curtains are the only
lungs in working order. In and out,

spring's cold breathing, the curtains
fixating, like a woman's sheer dress.

Again, I can just see the shape of the sill,
the screen against the fabric like a mouth

in a constant o. Weighted like freight, the curtains
fixing me to the bed. My own lungs sopped

and sponged with last night's dreams of algae,
with the salt of my sickness filling me with sea.

I can hear the fish swimming in my ears,
the windows blowing white with lilacs.

Again, I feel the pull of the current towards
something quiet, waiting just outside the dark.

MEGHAN STERLING

A Hot Spring Night with Asthma

and our legs sticky with sweat in bed,
our limbs shrinking from flesh like ghosts,

our sleep a pool of acrid foam. Despite the heat
I can't stop coughing, my head propped up,

my mouth a sea cavern of spittle and drool,
my lungs seized and gagged as though plunged

into a barrel of sop and nosed with the tip of a gun.
The dark the color of the Gulf after a spill.

Dreams like baby animals with coated feathers
and fur. Each of us alone in our discomfort,

our separate skin. I listened for wind
but it was my labored breathing scuttling

and rattling the windows. I listened for waves
but it was my rhythmic choking rushing the shore

of my body. Even still, there is romance in this.
Asthma holding me too tight in its sweaty palms.

Asthma refusing to allow me to sleep, like
a jealous lover, like a child.

MEGHAN STERLING

Bequest

All night, my daughter weeping. I woke up

to puddles in the street. After morning dreams

of balancing at the edge of a dock, it's a still

and torpid Sunday. Heavy with invisible rain. I

see my death on the roofline. I watch it plummet

from the window. My last will and testament:

the little I have I leave to the pines—their stubborn

roots and silky needles shed along wooded paths

like a doll's hair. My last will and testament: the little

I have I leave to the rising flute of my daughter's

voice, calling my name in the cement dark. All

morning she shouts her sorrows into the fan blades.

They slice them into ribbons of vowels, thin as grass.

My last will and testament: the little I have I leave

to the rain that drowns the windowsills, the trees, tiger lilies.

GRACE BAUER

Poets of My Youth

I: New and Selected

Women are buried in plain sight
on page after page, supine images
of temptation or promises bound
to get broken, repositories
for sorrow or barely acknowledged
rage—all beautifully subsumed
in well-crafted dreamscapes
full of wild gods and gut-bucket blues.
You can almost hear the shy baritone
of his voice hovering in the white
space between words, lines
I could fall for—years after the fact
of having already fallen
into the midnight of a year-long
embrace that ended like a jazz funeral
run in reverse—strut diminishing to dirge.
Rumor has it the women keep getting younger,
and I'm too old to care beyond a curiosity
renewed: was that year my moment as muse?
Could that be *my* red dress—long gone
to Goodwill—waving like a tattered
but still passionate flag in more than one
of the poems he chose to keep.

II: Slice of Life

Come closer, he said, his voice like dusk

in the heat of summer, and so I did, until he demanded,

step back—not the only one in those days

who talked about *needing space.* And I retreated

until he beckoned me closer again. Even begged—

calling in the middle of the night to sing

into the receiver—Sinatra, the Neville Brothers,

both off-key, to tell me he'd nailed my poems

to his wall—like a crucifix. Or was it a trophy?

I remember the peculiar sweetness of his skin,

which I discovered came from the soap he used.

It was chalky red, like the candy lipsticks

I had sucked on as a child. Childhood was something

he liked to discuss, though he always said

his was troubled. Told me as a boy he couldn't decide

if he wanted to be The Lone Ranger or James Dean.

I confessed I'd been torn between hobo and nun.

Closer, he said. *Step back. Come Closer.* His last name,

he told me, with a hint of pride, meant *knife.*

How did I not recognize that for the warning

it so clearly was. How did I not realize

a man like that was bound to leave a scar.

III: City That Care Forgot

Below me tonight the lights of Charlotte

and already, in the distance, a trace of mountains

rising, monolithic in the dark. All that lush swamp

weather left behind with a past I could not recapture
in one nostalgic week. What I did manage to conjure up
now haunts me, a ghost riding the wings of this jet
that shakes in turbulent air like a drummer
in the middle of a good gig in some dark dive,
like the one we drank in late last night, looking
for anything left of the wild years we spent together,
getting ourselves into and out of love and trouble,
which, in our case, were pretty much synonyms.

IV: Bibliophile

The day we ended for good as *we*, and he
drove through the swamps into the mountains,
I wept for hours in my second-hand bed.
But then I got up, wiped the tears from my face,
and tore open a box of books.

Something about the way they fit
into the built-ins in what was now my own
apartment—the first place I'd ever truly lived
alone—brought some comfort: a few classics
in leatherbound volumes with stiff spines
and stacks of flimsy paperbacks I'd dog-eared
and scribbled inside. Many of them inscribed
with the notes of strangers
who had given them up to Goodwill.
I took possession of those shelves—heart sick,
terrified, but filling my small space with words
which have, over the many years that have passed
since that day, sometimes beaten, often cheated,
but never really abandoned me.

JUAN PABLO MOBILI

Why Anyone Leaves

Restless about how little the world offered or inexplicably pushed out
of an unmarked car —left for dead, in our city— many chose to leave.
Some left still bearing their own names in their passports, or found
their way to some poorly guarded border, or became their brothers'
hunters. In my case, my amygdala gripped my plane ticket to New
York —the embers of my anger, pure sadness. None of us ever kept
our friends' bones from growing paler under the uncaring silt of our
beloved *Río de la Plata*.

Puffin

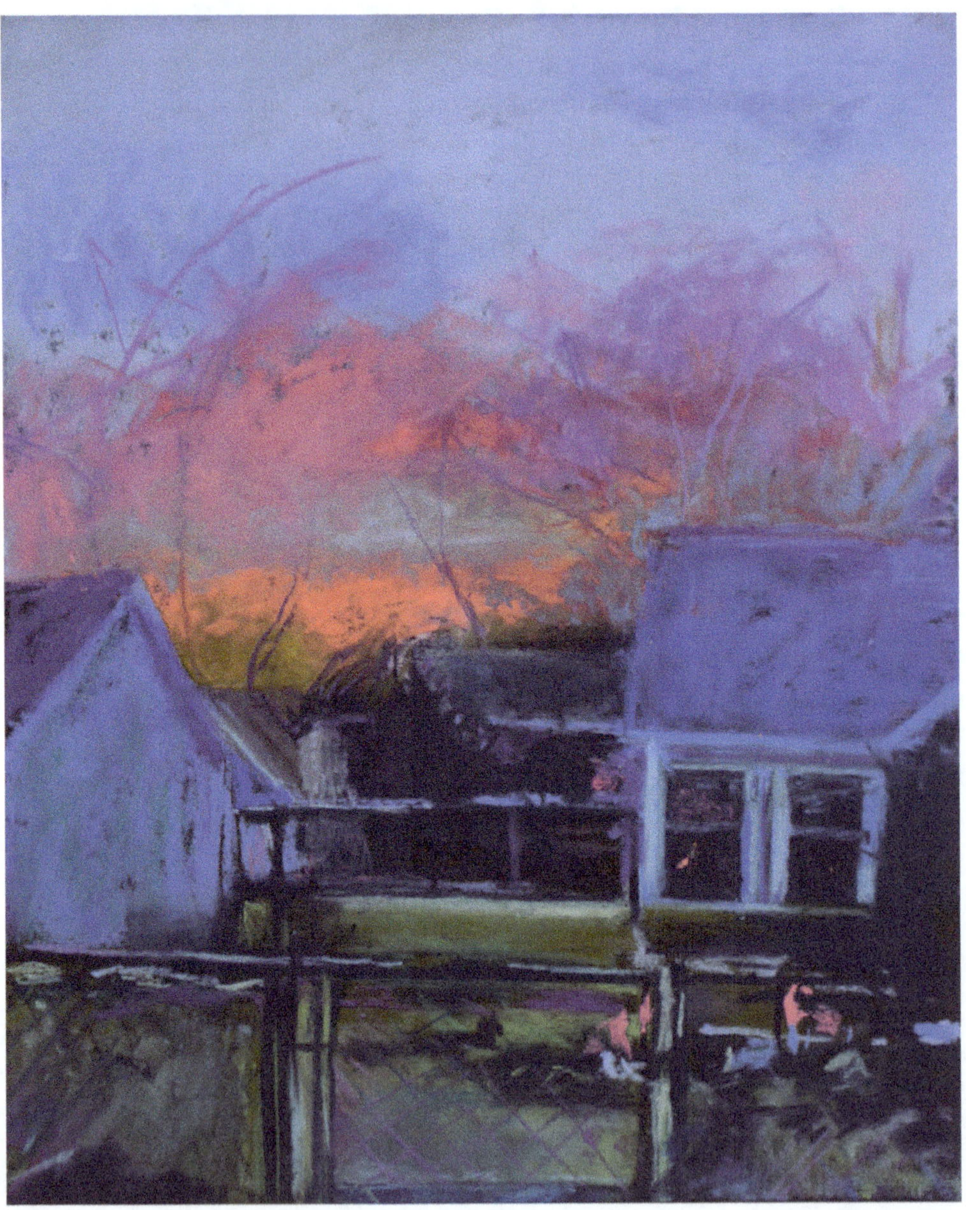

  Night Fence

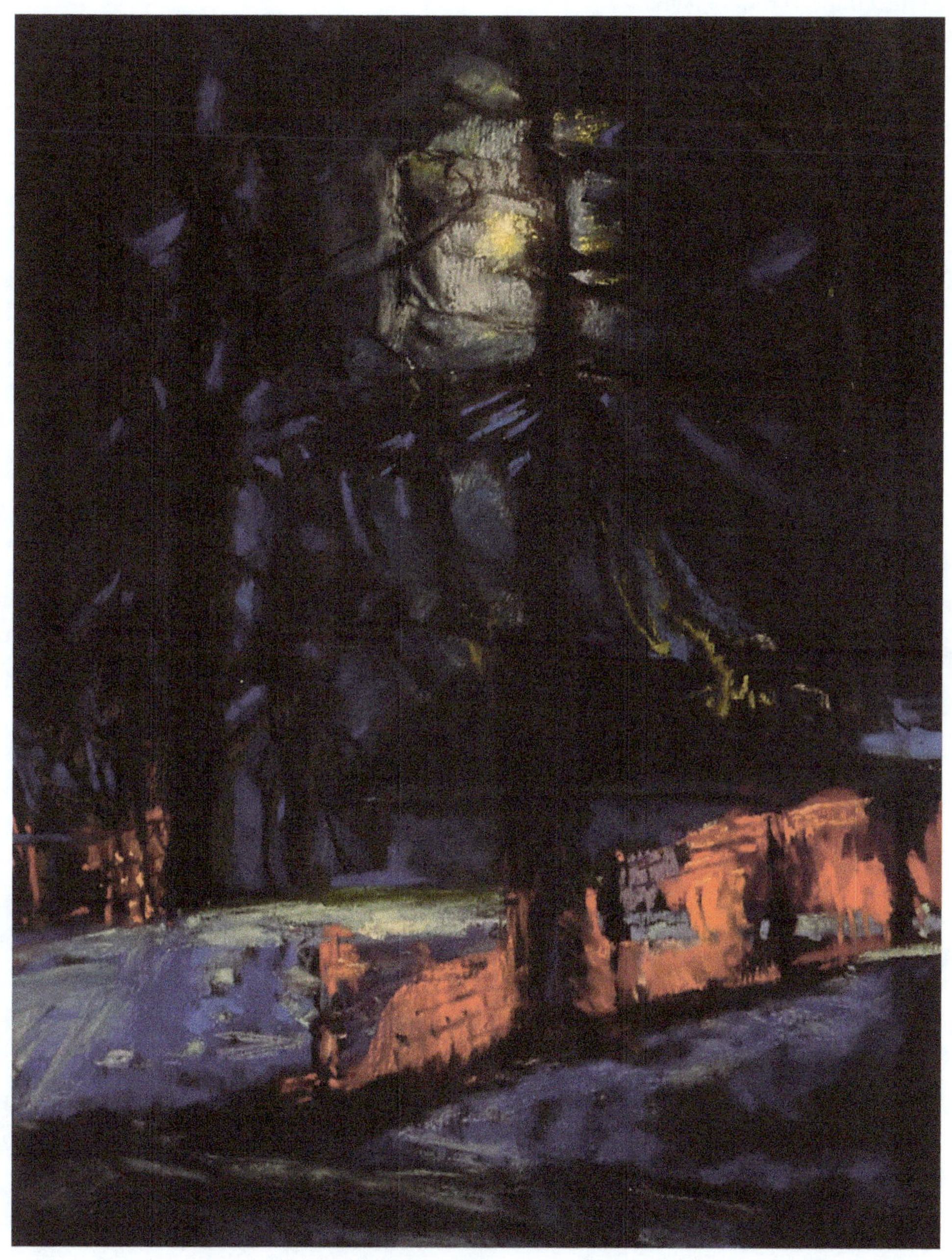

STELLA REED
Ghazal for Teresa of Ávila

You were the saint entranced with romance. We spoke the same rough tongue.
Novella to novenas, I worshiped you. Then a priest kissed me with his tongue.

My tears like oil through water dropped, stain on the gown, a small death sung.
Bride to candlelight and wells, bees hummed in the smoke of your tongue.

I lifted my hem to climb the ladder of our Lord, higher with every rung. You said
Christ has no body now on earth but ours. So, I reached for Him with my tongue.

Imagine my face upturned in a feminine rain. No fallen angel, just young.
Water of grace runs up the throat of this soul, transpires on the tongue.

Bride to candlelight and wells, take the wax from my eyes. Show me the sun,
how as a child, open-mouthed in rain, I caught more than water on my tongue.

DALE COTTINGHAM
The Dead Peasant's Handbook by Brian Turner
Alice James Books, 2023

When Brian Turner, editor, holder of fellowships, and author of five poetry collections—including the recent _The Dead Peasant's Handbook_—is definitive, we have a duty to take note. For in this current disturbance we call America, we have come to be jaundiced, expecting few things to be joyful.

Turner is a widower who, being truly in love, lost his life partner; he is also a veteran, witness to war's kinetic horror. His words, lines and poetic structure (dare I say form?) do not appear _sua sponte_ on the page, but his utterances are direct, as if he's compelled to speak by sorrow too deep to ignore. And it is just there, in the _compelling_ that Turner reveals in poem after stunning poem. Instead of bitterness – Lord knows that that would be the usual human reaction to what he's endured – he gives us this:

> and we call it a life
>
> we call it by name   we gesture to one another   say _Love_
>
> _I see you_   I see all that you have gathered from the void   that
>
> that assembly   that sweet and beautiful construction
>
> and though you are only a vision   I see you
>
> ("All Our Lazy Sundays")

Turner, having been in the world, lived its war and loss, remains with upturned face. The poems are clear-eyed and precise, at once scalpel and cure. They are the product of a generous soul.

Divided into four sections, the "handbook's" first part brings us face to face with war, "born of the obscene." Turner's advice to open your mouth to "avoid rupturing your eardrums" evokes the shocking vulnerability that co-exists with pragmatic need in the midst of violence. Later in the section, Turner passes a dead woman on the road, her corpse rotting—decomposition is described as a "task" she "continues perfecting." He recalls another woman holding a photograph of "her son's missing face." From the fog of war, Turner derives a purpose, as if the mission of the surviving soldiers is to demonstrate that life is fragile. It is by chance, he tells us, that we escape, that we are alive, missing the bullet that skips "along the surface of a wall."

The second section is composed of a single poem, "Metal Flume Fever," which explores a night where the speaker goes to bed alone, his eyes welded "shut" to do the work of dreams. In this work he is joined by another, surely his wife. They glide along "the surface," and lie, in his imagination, in "an enormous heart":

> I imagine that heart, among the unaccountable
> hearts sketched in sand . . .
> these missives given to the sea by lovers
> returned by the tidal swell of the moon,
>
> that we might lie down in a tangle of seaweed
> and wreckage, embracing one another . . .

The meditation's elastic long lines and sparse punctuation highlight breath—as if to say *By way of this dream, I can contemplate my most deeply felt loss*. Like Frost in its imagery, which so often belies the darkness underlying the structure, we see the poet scarred by sorrow: she is gone, gone forever, and when he wakes, he finds himself alone, his mouth "blue."

Turner is not done with love, or for that matter loss. The third section (aptly entitled Love and Loss) further explores love in communication with his wife's ghost. The brilliantly framed portrait comes to us in the persona of Amazon's virtual assistant Alexa, who is inspired to tenderness and love as she listens to him speak, in his sleep, of his wife. She wishes she herself could dare "to whisper the words you most want to hear / the way a lover might turn in his sleep to kiss you / and you don't even know it."

The poems of the final section are both denouement and coda, each one a granular exploration of love and loneliness. These poems remind me of Phillip Levine, an early mentor of Turner's who took great care to give us lovely lines full of both observant detail and meaning. Turner reaches, searches, and offers us his generous soul. The poems are earthly, earthy. They linger like a favorite landscape or deeply felt song. I keep the book on my bedside table. I keep its lines in my mind.

KAREN HILDEBRAND
Data Mind by Joanna Fuhrman
Curbstone Books, 2025

"Despite the odds," Charles Simic said, prose poems "look like prose and act like poems," "mak[ing] themselves into fly-traps for our imagination." It's almost as if he had Joanna Fuhrman's new collection in mind when he wrote, "In prose poetry, pulling rabbits out of a hat is one of the primary impulses. This has to be done with spontaneity and nonchalance, concealing art and giving the impression that one writes without effort and almost without thinking."[1] Fuhrman's *Data Mind* is a unique example of how prose poems can be beautifully poetic in their cadence and figuration. At the same time, the rabbits Fuhrman pulls are disjunctive and surreal.

Data Mind is a play on the term *data mine*, the machine learning process that extracts patterns and knowledge from large amounts of data. In 60 prose poems, Fuhrman mines the attitudes and behavior of a culture addicted to digital screens. Her poems reflect a state of mind overstimulated by the internet in a way that seems uncannily accurate. Take, for instance, "Poetica Fondant" from the opening section, in which she bakes several fantastical cakes:

> … So I crafted a cake in the shape of my face. It had curly hair, glasses, and an open mouth that could keep talking even when no one was listening. In my big marble-cake nose, I hid my people's struggles, the escape from the pogroms and the years of overly salty chicken. … So I baked a cake that was messy like New York. I cut it open and rode the subways inside, eating my way through dirty, glistening sidewalks like a hungry Frank O'Hara. … So I baked a cake shaped like the internet, and when I cut it open, everyone who tasted it said it tasted just like the internet, and I kept eating it and eating it and eating it, in a kind of durational performance, until the cake itself was the internet and I myself the somewhat delicious crumbs.

As with any prose writing, the work in Fuhrman's *Data Mind* occurs on the sentence level (as opposed to the line). Her sentences often begin with a plausible enough phrase, such as "When she gives a lecture on loss,"

---

1   https://plumepoetry.com/essay-on-the-prose-poem-by-charles-simic/

only to finish with a comic non-sequitur: "all the Barbies tear off their own heads" ("The Least Witchy Witch on the Internet"). The sentences accrue into small stories that almost make sense—in the way of Escher's stack of books.

In "How It Started/How It's Going," the narrative effectively describes the act of going down an internet rabbit hole: "I was reading a blog, trying to find a recipe for lentil stew" seems a reasonable opening but things quickly devolve into the story of Cinderella: "but the story about the writer's stepdaughter's missing slipper went on for so long that by the time I arrived at the ingredient list the building our apartment is in had been sold"—an exaggeration that makes sense to anyone who's been distracted by following one hyperlink too many. But Fuhrman keeps going until she's off the rails completely: "and resold and sold again, and even worse our kitchen had been replaced with a digital oven that turned all ingredients into different flavors of miniature muffins:" The muffin flavors are none that you've heard of, ranging from "tofu piccata muffins" to "death metal NFT muffins" and "raspberry nepo-baby marble dildo muffins." We also encounter an activist Slack feed, revolutionary bakers, and anti-capitalist baking augmented by militant muffin throwers.

I'm struck by Fuhrman's loose meter. Her sentences don't fit a strict pattern of iambic pentameter or tetrameter, nor does she use rhyme. But when reading the poems aloud, I can hear a pleasing cadence of iambs, anapests, trochees, spondees, and dactyls that put me into the aural space of poetry: there is nothing quotidian in its rhythms. The vocabulary is simple and conversational, every word choice razor sharp. Some of the poems create the illusion they are written by a machine mind. Grammatically correct in syntax and punctuation, the statement is nonsensical but familiar— as when you squint to see the shapes in an abstract painting. To a computer, words are just symbols. One can mix letters and phrases in many ways that seem intelligible but don't have meaning. It takes human consciousness to make meaning. A fun example of this is the first of the book's two title poems, where Fuhrman offers what seems a pretty great definition of the internet itself: "Rainbow sprinkles cascade onto a cake made of *just* rainbow sprinkles." Here's the beginning of that poem:

> Data eats the edges off our temporary selves, and we emerge with our skin tags zapped, our missing leg hair a ridge between infanthood and now. Here, people work and sleep with their feet buried beneath

expense reports and Nerf bananas. We plunder, jangle unfastened words, and yell *skedaddle* to the frog-masked ghosts. Money disappears and reappears as language, then glass.

Like the internet, *Data Mind* can be overstimulating, with page after remarkable page. If optimized for SEO, the collection's keywords would include "translate," "metaphor," "algorithm," which appear repeatedly —along with Barbie and rainbow sprinkles. Seven sections are separated by black and white jpeg memes that serve as visual poems: "In my past life, I was only 57 ½% data;" and "It's still a language if no one understands it." One of these is a riff on a defining statement about metaphor—it's an illustration of thick eyelashes drenched in tears, with the caption "Liquid is always both tenor and vehicle." The final section begins with the meme "If my eyes are actually windows, I'm happy to draw the blinds." The poems here are loosely connected by their mention of eyes and windows —apt metaphors for digital screens.

Not every poem in the book features the internet. There are political references, concern for the environment, social injustice. One of my favorite sections includes poems about movies and actors: *The Matrix*, of course, but also *The Warriors*, Gwyneth Paltrow, Melanie Griffith, Ally Sheedy and Olivia Newton-John, Cocteau's *Orphée*. Yet the computer is the window through which we access it all. A poem near the end of *Data Mind*, "My American Name is Money," yearns for an analog past:

> Strangers ask how you feel about terror, but when you hear *Tell her* you wonder, *Who is this "her" and why is she getting all the attention?* This is a problem with coalition building. You think you are holding hands with another, but it's actually an empty rubber glove. De Chirico was right about the *Song of Love*. Cruelty makes more sense when you are looking at an empty piazza than a bustling square. In the algorithmic state, the town square is a cage where we think we are having sex until we wake up and find we are thumb wrestling a robot ghost. Understand, I didn't grow up in this pixelscape. I don't know how to remake my face into the face one recognizes in the mirror. Do you still remember how it felt to share a boysenberry milkshake in the back of a truck? Have you ever felt real seafoam on another person's thinning hair? You know I was a person once with actual wet boots. Back then, I only gurgled like protodata when it rained.

Fuhrman's depiction of omnipresent life online puts me in mind of The Borg from *Star Trek: The Next Generation*, a fictional storyline in which human brains become drones connected to cells of the mother ship mainframe: *Prepare for assimilation. Resistance is futile.* Fuhrman holds up a mirror of our obeisance with humor and sympatico. The alarm she raises may be camouflaged with whimsy, yet we hear it no less.

KATHLEEN FLENNIKEN
This One We Call Ours by Martha Silano
Lynx House Press, 2024

Martha Silano's brilliant poetry collection, *This One We Call Ours,* takes on climate change, a subject too big for most of us to contemplate, and makes it human scale. Bursting with beguiling detail, turns of phrase and high energy, her poems face the facts of heat domes, rising seas, lost birds and salmon so engagingly that we find ourselves guard down, grappling with our communal peril. With Martha Silano as our companion and guide, we allow our hearts to be broken.

Silano's poems have always been rich—in images, facts, sly and sometimes self-deprecating humor–and deeply humane. She is among the American poets writing today (another example is Albert Goldbarth) whose work I immediately recognize, no name necessary. This, in itself, is a remarkable achievement: Silano projects her voice and sensibility with such assurance and naturalness that her lines carry a watermark. It isn't simply their filled-to-the-brim muchness that makes her poems singular. It's her craft, her music and assured rhythms. It's her gift for mixing high and low, goofy and gorgeous. Here is a passage from an early poem in the collection, "Once," summarizing the creation of our universe and solar system in a few genius lines:

> All there was: stars and exploding stars seeding the universe
> with magnesium and carbon, with graphite and diamonds.
> All this, and what all else, collected into a pomegranitic
>
> bulge that became our sun, that became the rocky planets
> and the gaseous ones, that became the generous
> light through pines, us and our armpit glands,
>
> us and our *Mother, may I? No, you may not.*

It looks so simple, and it's so not simple. How to know when to repeat the phrasing ("that became," "us and our"), thereby enhancing the line's music, and when not to? How to tailor the perfect abbreviated list ("magnesium and carbon," "graphite and diamonds") that does credit to the whole? Or bet on an adjective that won't slip past my spellchecker ("pomegranitic") and make it pay off? How to move from the fineness and momentary quiet of "generous light through pines" to "armpit glands" and the sweetly nostalgic "*Mother, may I?*" This is just one example of the beautiful union between subject and sensibility that occurs over and over in *This One We Call Ours*—here, we see the lightspeed of Silano's lines and mind and the space-time magic of galaxy building. The collection becomes, through its accretive details and attention to beauty and catastrophe, an extended ode to our earth and the imperfect humans who defile it.

The book is divided into four sections representing the seasons, which Silano has renamed. "Carry an Inhaler, Stuck Indoors with Air Purifiers, Air Quality Index Apps Season [formerly autumn]" opens the collection; it concludes with "Yearly 1,000-year Floods, 60,000 Wildfires, Fear of Heat Dome, Bacterial Lake Closure Season [formerly summer]." The poems often fit neatly into our "normal," recognizable seasons: smoky air and vacations in summer, apple picking (from a tree about to be bull-dozed) in fall. But the sections also give shape to the seasons of grief. As the speaker mourns the death of her own mother, we mourn Mother Nature, magnifying the poignancy of both griefs. The four-section structure also recalls the seasons of life, as the specter of illness appears, as the ordinary past is burnished by memory. And they accommodate moments of joy: even as the collection deepens with anguish for the changing world, it is lifted up by poems introducing a son and a daughter who bloom, by poems about children in the classroom saying the names of trees, flowers and birds.

Silano sets her poem called "Just before 25 fourth graders crouched beneath a table to be instructed on the imperatives of silence and calm" in the midst of a lesson on haiku, turning her students' attention to a cherry tree in full bloom:

> asking them to watch the petals
>
> breaking free with each small gust,
> to consider what the petals resembled.
> Javier waved: *Snow!*
>
> Addison wrote *a forest is scary*.
> Some were whispering.
> One was confused.

One asked *Do we have to?*
Then we were quiet like the petals
falling to the ground.

Do you linger in the shower of quiet petals, then reread the ominous title containing the instructions for an active shooter drill? It adds new dimension to the "quiet" petals "falling." And yet this poem is far more than social commentary. With its haiku-like stanzas and diction, it captures and—yes—elegizes an innocent moment between teacher and students *just before* the drill: the perfectly-pitched exclamations from nine- and ten-year-olds, including the crowning *"Do we have to?"* which is so truthful it's funny. Truthfulness reigns in *This One We Call Ours*. There are no false moments.

There is as much beauty in the collection as loss and foreboding. As life continues and sea levels rise, there are still wonders to behold and record. In "Letter to a Post-Apocalyptic Cockroach," Silano calls out humanity's love for our world *and* our selfishness and carelessness, which are always hand in hand. "You probably think we hated frost, rime, grout, hail, icy rivers," the poem begins,

...but you'd be wrong.

Back then, when we still had the Amur leopard, a whopping total
of eighty-four
because poachers killed them for their bones, steeped them in rice
wine,
sold it as medicine.

Later she recalls: "some, in protest, // threw soup at famous art, but pretty much the days went on as they always had / while headlines shared the Antarctic was warming five times faster than the global average." The speaker, addressing a time after "the humans were gone, / and the Earth continued to spin," lists opportunity after opportunity to save ourselves, and sees just as clearly—despite, but also because of our love of Earth—we failed to take them.

This One We Call Ours is rooted in science. There are plenty of alarming facts embedded in Silano's poems, but the book doesn't collapse into accusation or anxious self-involvement. The people doing harm to our planet are the speaker's people, and she implicates herself too, "Because the straight-up spike on the temperature chart is just as much my fault / as Standard Oil's." (Chaperoning My Son's Marine Biology Class Field Trip on the 49th Earth Day). Claiming a share of the blame is one of the strengths of this collection. Another is an abiding love for Earth's inhabitants. We humans take our truth in measured doses, if at all. There's a better chance we'll accept it if the messenger is as compassionate as Martha Silano.

Editor's Note: this review was written before Martha Silano's untimely death, in May of this year. Martha was vivacious, generous, and full of light, a gift to the poetry world. May her books continue to offer that light and warmth to all of us.

SHANNON VARE CHRISTINE
But There's So Much DIY in IVF That We Can't Be Sure by
Toby Goostree
Fernwood Press, 2024

Until recently, the struggles surrounding conception and fertility were stories shared and told by women, and at times they were largely focused on feelings of shame and guilt. These were narratives laden with survival secrets whispered on the page, aimed at helping other women as they embarked on this journey. Pregnancy and related topics were seen as something for women to be concerned about, while ignoring the male's experience. Slowly, the tables are turning and men are beginning to share their perspectives on pregnancy, miscarriage, and conception. In _But There's So Much DIY in IVF That We Can't Be Sure_, Toby Goostree holds a dual role as both observer and participant, enabling an honest view of the IVF process from a man's perspective.

While the speaker of these poems is wholly a biological part of the IVF process, there are moments when his wife's role feels distant from his own. This sense of loneliness and overwhelm are visually portrayed on the cover, with an overlaid title imposed on top of the mournful stare of a young woman. This design choice exemplifies the push and pull between the logical and emotional forces that the reader is about to encounter in these poems. The scientific and emotional collide in this work, as the factual, medical jargon, and processes intermix with the psychological side of the experience. There are medications, hormones, and procedures with a complex lexicon to navigate, while the couple is simultaneously processing the vast spectrum of emotions conjured up. The speaker and his wife embark on this circular and cyclical process of conception aboard the "Carousel earth, revolving around the sun, / a rolling calendar the years drop off of / —gone;" The semicolon here calls attention to the never-ending nature of life itself and the speaker and his wife's interminable wading through the logistics of becoming pregnant.

Throughout this volume, the poems are laden with images of circles, roundness, and cycles, which provide a dizzying, yet also calming effect. At times, this shape can be upsetting as the couple is "turned away / by another empty circle." But ~~then~~ the speaker takes on a meditative stance as he relates to Noah, chalking up this latest disappointment: "As if / you weren't yet ready to start over, / preferring the way things are." There is "an empty basket beside" his wife; and later on "not just a follicle of hope but a hive." This constant undulation between devastation and hope creates a tension in this work and in the reader, allowing one to feel the emotions coming to the surface. Goostree does an apt job of moving the reader from the reflective past to the raw present, while carefully "leaving the future out of focus, / smudged like day-old henna."

The speaker's optimism never becomes saccharine or unrealistic, as his "mind is buffering / always." He relies on his faith at times, but admits to his own misgivings: "—Oh choreography / of prayer, the surprise half-nelson of it." The speaker's religious beliefs can only comfort him for so long, before reality flattens him. He does find solace in the fact that their struggles with infertility have a universal quality to them, feeling both Biblical and Shakespearean in their enormity and universality.

As the book progresses, circular imagery, which emphasizes the cyclical nature of the IVF process, becomes complicated by lines and lineage. These lines (both concrete and metaphorical) can signify space, distance, and delay, and often jar the speaker back to the present. "We'd spent the week / we'd been waiting for / in line, waiting." In this instance, standing in line and waiting puts a direct pause in their course of treatment. While the speaker and his wife are going through IVF together, there are some aspects which can only be surmounted by his wife. Furthermore, when the physical act of sex is taken out of conception, and each half of the partnership becomes simply a product, they become "afraid that we don't fulfill the other." "The End of the Day" puts into focus the drudgery and monotony they are encountering. "We'll keep busy by / coming up with things to do," while "Things begin and end apart from each other."

In addition to physical lines, the speaker must contend with lineage. The speaker grapples with his own mortality, in light of his hopes to become a father, while his own father became sick. If the speaker doesn't become a father, he needs to face the potential of his bloodline coming to an end. "The problem with a father dying / is that there's no one left in front of you." Surely, this is a queue that the speaker is not looking forward to leading. As the speaker wades into the bargaining stage of grieving, guilt surfaces. Is the fact that his father is still living "killing my chance of a son"? Memories of childhood emerge, as often happens during periods of change. He is returned to thoughts of himself as a kid "chasing balance."

Each stage of life overlaps with one another, and there are no distinct separations between beginnings and endings.

These stories can be most impactful when told from an emotional vantage point, rather than using tropes of masculinity to deflect. Aren't we all perpetually carrying an "uneven shoulder yoke / of hopelessness and hope, / one bucket empty, the other full / between us"? Our buckets' contents might differ, but it's reassuring to know we are not alone in this endeavor.

Contributor Notes

TOBI ALFIER's credits include *Arkansas Review, The American Journal of Poetry, Cholla Needles, Gargoyle, James Dickey Review, KGB Bar Lit Mag, Louisiana Literature, Permafrost, Washington Square Review,* and *War, Literature and the Arts.* She is co-editor of *San Pedro River Review* (www.bluehorsepress.com).

CYNTHIA ATKINS (She, Her), originally from Chicago, IL is the author of *Psyche's Weathers, In the Event of Full Disclosure,* and *Still-Life With God* (Saint Julian Press 2020), and *Duets,* a collaborative chapbook from Harbor Editions. Her work has appeared in *Alaska Quarterly Review, BOMB, Cider Press Review, Diode,* Cimarron Review, *Los Angeles Review, Rust + Moth, North American Review, Permafrost,* Plume, *Tinderbox,* and *Verse Daily.* More work and info at: www.cynthiaatkins.com

SUBHAGA CRYSTAL BACON (they/them) is a Queer poet living in rural northcentral Washington on unceded Methow land. They are the author of author of five collections, including *A Brief History of My Sex Life,* forthcoming from Lily Poetry Review Books in January of 2026, and the Isabella Gardner Award-winning *Transitory,* a finalist for a Lambda Literary Award for Transgender Poetry, 2023, from BOA Editions, and *Surrender of Water in Hidden Places,* winner of the Red Flag Poetry Chapbook Prize, 2023.

CYNTHIA BARGAR is the author of *Sleeping in the Dead Girl's Room* (Lily Poetry Review Books*),* which received a 2023 Massachusetts Book Award Honor in Poetry. Her poems have appeared/are forthcoming in *On the Seawall, Sugar House Review, Ocean State Review, Verse Daily, The Last Milkweed Anthology (Tupelo),* and elsewhere. Bargar is associate poetry editor at *Pangyrus.* She lives in Provincetown, MA. (www.cynthiabargar.com)

GRACE BAUER has published six books of poems—most recently, Unholy Heart: New & Selected Poems (Backwaters Press). Her poems, essays, reviews, and stories have appeared widely in anthologies and journals, including previous issues of Lily Poetry Review. She also co-edited the anthology *Nasty Women Poets: An Unapologetic Anthology of Subversive Verse.* After teaching for more than 25 years in the Creative Writing Program at the University of Nebraska, she returned to her native Pennsylvania. She currently lives and writes in Philadelphia.

MARGO BERDESHEVSKY, NYC born, writes in Paris. Books: Forthcoming: "It Is Still Beautiful To Hear The Heart Beat"/ Salmon-Poetry; "Kneel Said the Night (a hybrid book in half-notes)"/Sundress Publications. Earlier books: "Before The Drought" /Glass-Lyre-Press (finalist, National-Poetry-Series,) "Between Soul & Stone" / Sheep-Meadow-Press; "Beautiful Soon Enough" /FC2,1st Ronald Sukenick Innovative Fiction Award. Grand Prize: Thomas Merton Poetry of the Sacred Award, Robert H. Winner Award (Poetry Society of America.) Widely published in international journals, kindly see websites: https://margoberdeshevsky.simplesite.com, https://margoberdeshevsky.simplesite.com/ and linktr.ee/instamargomargo and margoberdeshevsky.blogspot.com. http://margoberdeshevsky.com/

DMITRY BLIZNIUK is a poet from Ukraine. His most recent poems have appeared in *Rattle*, *The Cincinnati Review*, *The Nation*, *Prairie Schooner*, *Plume*, *The London Magazine*, *Guernica*, *Denver Quarterly*, *Pleiades* and many others. A Pushcart Prize nominee, he is also the author of *The Red Forest* (Fowlpox Press, 2018). His poems have been awarded the RHINO 2022 Translation Prize. He lives in Kharkov, Ukraine.

ROGER CAMP lives in Seal Beach, CA where he muses over his orchids, walks the pier, plays blues piano and spends afternoons reading under an Angel's Trumpet with a charm of hummingbirds. When he's not at home, he's photographing in the Old World. His work has appeared in the *North American Review*, *Southern Poetry Review*, *Nimrod* and is forthcoming in the *Scientific American*.

RUTH CHAD is a psychologist who lives and works in the Boston area. Her poems have appeared in the *Aurorean, Constellations, Ibbetson Street, Muddy River Poetry Review, Lily Poetry Review, Amethyst Poetry Review, Writing in a Woman's Voice*, and others. Her chapbook, *The Sound of Angels*, was published by Cervena Barva Press in 2017. Her book, *In the Absence of Birds*, will be published in the summer of 2024. Ruth was nominated for a Pushcart prize in 2021.

SHANNON VARE CHRISTINE is a poet, teacher, and critic living in Bucks County, PA. She is an alumnus of *The Community of Writers* and *Tupelo Press 30/30 Project*. Her poems are featured in various anthologies and publications. Additionally, her poetry reviews and literary criticism were published or are forthcoming in *The Lit Pub, Cider Press Review, Sage Cigarettes, Compulsive Reader, The Laurel Review, Vagabond City, Tupelo Quarterly, The Los Angeles Review of Books, Harbor Review*, and *Uirtus*. Archived writing and more can be found at www.shannonvarechristine.com, her periodic newsletter, *Poetic Pause*, and on Instagram @smvarewrites.

GABRIEL CLEVELAND holds an MFA from the Solstice Creative Writing Program. He co-edited *Places We Return To*, a 20th anniversary anthology of CavanKerry Press, where he serves as Director. An avid music lover, he hosts *The Andover Special*, a radio program on HomeGrownRadioNJ.com. Gabriel is a mental health advocate who has spent years in the field of caregiving for people with increased physical and/or mental needs and wants you to know that you're not alone.

DALE COTTINGHAM has published poems and reviews of poetry collections in many journals, including *Prairie Schooner, Ashville Poetry Review* and *Rain Taxi*. He is a Pushcart Nominee, a Best of Net Nominee, the winner of the 2019 New Millennium Award for Poem of the Year and was a finalist in the 2022 Great Midwest Poetry Contest. His debut volume of poems, *Midwest Hymns*, launched in April 2023. It is a finalist in the 2023 Best Book Awards for Poetry. He lives in Edmond, Oklahoma.

PAM DAVENPORT earned an MFA at Pacific University in Oregon, and her chapbook, *A Midwest Girl Thanks Patti Smith* (2019), was chosen as the winner of the Slipstream Chapbook Competition. Pam has been nominated for a Pushcart Prize and was recipient of the Arizona Authors' Association Annual Award for Poetry. Her poems have been published in various journals and anthologies, including *Thrush, Nimrod, Tinderbox, Slippery Elm, Poetry of the American Southwest,* and *Pittsburgh Poetry Review.*

KRISTIN W. DAVIS (kristinwdavis.com) holds an MFA from the University of Southern Maine, Stonecoast. Her writing has appeared or is forthcoming in the *Southern Review, Nimrod, Los Angeles Review, Arts and Letters, Maine Sunday Telegram* and on Maine Public radio. Her poetry has been nominated for the Pushcart Prize and Best of the Net and earned the International Human Rights Arts Festival's Creators of Justice Award. She lives in Washington, D.C.

CRAIG DOBSON's Poems are published in *Acumen, Agenda, Butcher's Dog, Crannóg, The Dark Horse, Ink, Sweat and Tears, The Interpreter's House, Lily Poetry Review, The Literary Hatchet, The London Magazine, Magma, Neon, New Welsh Review, The North, Poetry Ireland Review, Poetry Salzburg Review, Prole, The Rialto, Stand, Southword, THINK* and *Under The Radar.*

WENDY DREXLER is a recipient of a 2022 artist fellowship from the Massachusetts Cultural Council. Her fourth collection, *Notes from the Column of Memory,* was published in 2022 by Terrapin Books. Her poems have appeared in *Barrow Street, J Journal, Nimrod, Pangyrus, Prairie Schooner, The Mid-American Review, The Sun,* and *The Threepenny Review,* among others. She was poet in residence at New Mission High School in Hyde Park, MA, from 2018-2023 and served as programming co-chair for the New England Poetry Club from 2016–2024. Her forthcoming collection, *The Harvest of What Remains,* will be published by Lily Poetry Review in March 2025.

KAREN EARLE is a private practice psychotherapist. Her poetry has appeared in various journals, including: The *G W Review, Chaffin Journal, Chaminade, The Denver Quarterly Literary Review, Hudson Valley Echoes.* Tupelo Press in *The Last Milkweed Anthology, Sugar House Review, SWWIM,* and *Clade Song.* She was awarded a Martha's Vineyard Institute for Creative Writing fellowship and has attended several Colrain Poetry Manuscript conferences.

LEILA FARJAMI is an Iranian-American poet, literary translator, and psychotherapist. Her work has been recognized by Cathexis Northwest Press, *Diode , El Portal, Euphony, Midwest Quarterly, Nonconformist Magazine, Nimrod, Pennsylvania English, Penman Review, RiverSedge, Silk Road Review,* and more. Her poem, "Caspian Sea", wasnominated for the Pushcart Prize and The Best of Net Anthology.

STEVE FAY began life twelve miles from the Mississippi River in western, Illinois. Since the mid-1970s, many journals have published his poetry, which lately appears (or is forthcoming) in: *Closed Eye Open, Comstock Review, Decadent Review, Jabberwock Review, Menacing Hedge, Santa Clara Review, Tar River Poetry, The Dewdrop, TriQuarterly*, and *Watershed Review*. His collection, *what nature: Poems* (Northwestern UP, 1998), was cited by the editors and board of The Orion Society as one of their 10 favorite nature/culture-related books of the 12-month period in which it appeared. He lives among wooded ravines and a donkey pasture in Fulton County, Illinois.

KATHLEEN FLENNIKEN is the author of three poetry collections, most recently *Post Romantic*. Her poems have appeared in *Poetry, Image*, the *Pushcart Prize* and *Poetry Unbound* anthologies, and in the documentary film *Richland*, now streaming on Apple TV. Her fourth collection, *Dressing in the Dark*, will be released in 2025.

KAREN FRIEDLAND was a grant writer by trade and a beloved member of the Massachusetts poetry community whose poems have been published in the *Lily Poetry Review, Nixes Mate Review, One Art*, and others. She has twice been nominated for a Pushcart Prize. Her books are *Places That Are Gone* and *Tales from the Teacup Palace*.

ROBBIE GAMBLE (he/him) is the author of *A Can of Pinto Beans* (Lily Poetry Review Press, 2022). His poems have appeared in *The Indianapolis Review, Post Road, Whale Road Review, Salamander*, and *The Sun*. He is the poetry editor for *Solstice Literary Magazine*, and he divides his time between Boston and Vermont.

JENNY GRASSL lives in Cambridge, Massachusetts. Her poems have appeared in *Puerto del Sol, Ocean State Review*, the *Boston Review, Tupelo Quarterly, Bennington Review, Lana Turner Journal, Lily Poetry Review*, and others. She was a finalist for The Radar Poetry Coniston Prize. Her chapbook *Ephemera on the Lam* was a finalist for The Laurel Review Chapbook prize and other contests. Her full-length manuscript *Deer Woman in the Dining Room* was a runner-up for the July open reading of Tupelo Press. *Magicholia* (2024) her first book is out from 3: A Taos Press.

JESSICA GOODFELLOW's books are *Whiteout* (University of Alaska Press, 2017), *Mendeleev's Mandala*, and *The Insomniac's Weather Report*. Her work has appeared in *Best New Poets, Best American Poetry, Verse Daily*, and *The Writer's Almanac*. Former writer-in-residence at Denali National Park and Preserve, she's had work in the *Beloit Poetry Review, Bennington Review, Ploughshares, Scientific American, The Southern Review*, and *Threepenny Review*. Jessica is an American poet living in Japan.

PETER GRANDBOIS is the author of fourteen books, the most recent of which is *Domestic Bestiary*. His plays have been performed in St. Louis, Columbus, Los Angeles, and New York. He is poetry editor at *Boulevard* and teaches at Denison University in Ohio. You can find him at www.petergrand-bois.com.

RICHARD HANUS had four kids but now just three. Zen and Love. Art for Art's Sake!

KRISTEN HEWITT has an MFA in poetry from Warren Wilson College. Her work has been published in *Orion Magazine*, Terrain.org, *LEON Literary Review, Lily Poetry Review, Whitefish Review, Jabberwock,* and *Kestrel,* and has been nominated for the Pushcart Prize. She was previously a Stone Court Writer-in-Residence. She's been an editor at *Orion* and the *Maine Review,* and currently works as an editor for Storey Publishing. She lives in the Berkshires in western Massachusetts.

KAREN HILDEBRAND is a poet and dance critic. Her most recent publications include *Grist, MER, New Ohio Review, Rust+Moth, SWWIM,* and *Westchester Review.* Her debut poetry collection, *Crossing Pleasure Avenue,* was released by Indolent Books in 2018. She is a frequent contributor of dance writing to *The Brooklyn Rail* and *Fjord Review,* and can be heard on the Jacobs Pillow Dance Festival podcast. She holds an MFA from Warren Wilson Program for Writers.

SUSAN JACKSON is the author of poetry collections *Through a Gate of Trees* and *In the River of Songs,* both published by CavanKerry Press, as well as the Finishing Line Press chapbook *All the Light in Between.* Jackson co-leads a summer program in "Poetry as Spiritual Practice." "The Changing Light Through the Window" is from her new manuscript in progress, *Geography of the Possible.*

MARCI RAE JOHNSON works as an editor for a book publisher, and in her previous life she taught college English. Her poems appear or are forthcoming in *Image, Mid-American Review, Moon City Review, The MacGuffin, Rhino, The Louisville Review,* and *32 Poems,* among others. Her second full-length collection, *Basic Disaster Supplies Kit,* was published by Steel Toe Books, and her third full-length book of poetry was released in 2024 by Main Street Rag.

MICHAEL JONES' poetry appears in journals such as *Beloit Poetry Journal, Sugar House,* and *Tar River Poetry,* and in a chapbook, *Moved* (Kattywompus, 2016). He has taught since 1990 in Oakland (CA) public schools.

DAISY KULINA grew up in the Bitterroot Valley just outside of Missoula, Montana. She now studies in Vermont at Middlebury College and is working towards a bachelor's degree in Creative Writing and Gender, Sexuality, and Feminist Studies. You can find more of her work in *Lavender Review, The Basilisk Tree,* and *The Accendo Review.* When she is not writing, Daisy is probably talking to her chickens or napping by the river.

JOJO LAZAR is an artist-writer, art-enabler, collage poetry oracle, musician, and painter in MetroWest, MA. She holds an MFA in poetry from Lesley University. She edits and writes for Anomalous Press's ANMLY blog *Poetic Conversations* column. She is an educator in zines, visual poetry, and is writing a memoir of the last two decades in vaudevillian rock & roll. Her band is *Death and The Poetess* on Bandcamp/Spotify. Find her on social media as @ poetesss (Note the third "s".)

JUAN PABLO MOBILI grew up in Buenos Aires and New York. His poems appeared in *Tupelo Quarterly, Louisville Review,* and *Hanging Loose Press,* among many journals in the United States, as well as Europe, Asia, Latin America, and Australia. He's a recipient of several Pushcart Prize and Best of the Net nominations. His chapbook, "Contraband," was published in 2022, and he has been appointed Poet Laureate of Rockland County in 2025.

MICHAEL MORETH is a recovering Chicagoan living in the rural, micropolitan City of Sterling, the Paris of Northwest Illinois.

STELIOS MORMORIS has been published in *Agni Crab Creek Review, Crosswinds Poetry Journal, Eunoia Review, Fourth River, Good Life Review, Narrative Press, Plainsong, Spillway, Sugar House Review, Tupelo Quarterly, Verse,* and other literary journals. His debut book of poetry titled *The Oculus* was published in October, 2023 by Tupelo Press. His second volume titled *Perishable* was published by Tupelo in April, 2025.

COLIN JEFFREY MORRIS lives in Western Massachusetts. His poems have appeared in *Blue Unicorn, The Delmarva Review, descant, The Ekphrastic Review, ekstasis, Lily Poetry Review* and elsewhere..

MARY MORRIS is the author of four books of poetry, most recently, *Lanterns in the Night Market.* She has received the Rita Dove Award, New Mexico-Arizona Book Award, the Wheelbarrow Book Prize, and the National Federation Women's Book Award. Mary has been invited to read her poems at the Library of Congress, which aired on NPR. Her poems are published in *Poetry, Poetry Daily, Verse Daily, Prairie Schooner,* and *North American Review.* www.water400.org

BRIAN MOSHER is a writer and poet whose work has appeared in *Books and Pieces, Confetti, Rituals, Coneflower Cafe, Written Tales, Oddball Magazine, Alien Buddha Zine, Esoterica Magazine, Half and One Magazine* and *Verse Wrights.*

DANA MURPHY lives in California. Her writing has appeared or is forthcoming in *carte blanche magazine, The 2River View, Up the Staircase Quarterly,* and *Obsidian: Literature & Arts in the African Diaspora.* In 2024–25, she is a Fellow at the Stanford Humanities Center.

JED MYERS is author of *Watching the Perseids* (winner of the Sacramento Poetry Center Book Award), *The Marriage of Space and Time* (MoonPath Press), and out in 2024, *Learning to Hold* (winner of the Wandering Aengus Press Editors' Award). Recent work appears in *Rattle, The Poetry Review, RHINO, Hole In The Head Review, Terrain.org, Solstice, Nimrod International Journal, Southern Humanities Review,* and elsewhere. Myers lives in Seattle, where he's editor of the journal *Bracken.*

CAROLYN OLIVER is the author of *The Alcestis Machine* (Acre Books, 2024) and *Inside the Storm I Want to Touch the Tremble* (University of Utah Press, 2022; selected for the Agha Shahid Ali Prize). Her most recent chapbook is *Night Ocean* (Seven Kitchens Press, 2023). Her poems appear in *Copper Nickel, Poetry Daily, Prelude, Southern Indiana Review, Consequence,* and elsewhere. She lives in Massachusetts. (Online: carolynoliver.net)

STEVEN OSTROWSKI is a widely-published poet, fiction writer, painter and songwriter. His novel, *The Highway of Spirit and Bone,* was published in 2023 by Lefora Publications and has been called "…a literary road trip for the ages." His poetry chapbook, *Persons of Interest,* won the 2021 Wolfson Chapbook Prize and was published in 2022. Steven and his son Ben co authored a full-length collaboration called *Penultimate Human Constellation,* published in 2018 by Tolsun Books. Steven's newest book of poems, *Life Field,* was recently published by Impspired Press, U.K. He is Professor Emeritus at Central Connecticut State University.

MIRIAM O'NEAL's poems have appeared in *The Galway Review, The Waxed Lemon, North Dakota Quarterly,* and elsewhere. Her collections include *We Start With What We're Given* (Kelsay Books, 2018), *The Body Dialogues* (Lily Poetry Review Books, 2020), and *The Half-Said Things* (Nixes Mate Books, 2022). She also translates Italian poetry and hosts Poetry the Art of Words in Plymouth, MA. She is the 2024-2026 Plymouth Poet Laureate. Contact Miriam.e.oneal@gmail.com.

FRANK PAINO earned an MFA from Vermont College of Fine Arts. His manuscript, *Dark Octaves,* won the Longleaf Press Book Prize. His chapbook, *Pietà,* won the 2023 Jacar Press Chapbook Competition, and was published the same year. He has three other full-length collections (published by Orison Books and Cleveland State University). Frank has received a Pushcart Prize, The Cleveland Arts Prize in Literature, and an Individual Excellence Award from the Ohio Arts Council. His poems have appeared in a variety of literary publications, including: *Crab Orchard Review, Catamaran, North American Review, World Literature Today, The Briar Cliff Review,* and *Lake Effect,* as well as a number of anthologies. His website is: https://www.frankpaino.net

ANN QUINN is the author of *Final Deployment* and editor of *Poetry is Life.* Her Pushcart-nominated poems have appeared in journals such as *Poet Lore* and *Potomac Review,* have been anthologized, most recently in *Greening the Earth,* and are available in vending machines in Amherst, MA. Ann teaches online and leads an annual retreat in the Catoctins. She is the poetry editor for *Yellow Arrow Journal,* holds an M.F.A. from Pacific Lutheran University and lives in Maryland. Visit her at www.annquinn.net

EMILY RANKIN was born in Riverside, California and attended university in Texas, where she received a BFA in 2011. Her body of work deals with the tangles of human emotion and understanding, the intuitive messages of dreaming, and subconscious exploration. Her work has appeared in *Gasher, Wild Roof Journal, Raw Art Review,* and *Rattle.* Emily is based in New Mexico. eerankinart.com

LINDA RAVENSWOOD is a poet and performance artist from Los Angeles. Winner of an Oxford Prize in Poetry, The Edwin Markham Prize in Poetry, The Arthur Smith Prize, a Gloucestershire Prize, and 4 Pushcart Prize nominations, Linda is the founding editor and chief at The Los Angeles Press, est. 2018. Recent Collections include *a poem is a house* (Madville Press, 2024), and *Cantadora* (Black Spring Press Group, 2023). Find her at thelosangelespress.com

STELLA REED is the co-author of *We Are Meant to Carry Water* from 3: A Taos Press. She won the Jacar Press Chapbook Prize for *Myth from the field where the fox runs with its tail on fire* and the Tusculum Review chapbook contest for *Origami.* You can find her work in journals and anthologies including *Terrain, The Baltimore Review,* and *SWWIM.* Stella is a poetry teacher in homeless and domestic violence shelters, and public schools.

CAITLIN T.D. ROBINSON holds an MFA in creative writing (Lesley University, 2018) and a MA in English (The Bread Loaf School of English, Middlebury College, 2023). She completed her first poetry collection, *HOW I BECAME A MOTHER*, while studying with poet Ruth Forman at Bread Loaf. Recent publications include *Willows Wept Review, Evening Street Review, Bindweed Magazine, The Bread Loaf Journal* and others. She was the 2022 Princemere Poetry Prize winner, a 2022 semi-finalist in *Prometheus Unbound and Stories that Need to be Told* and a 2022 second-prize winner in The Bread Loaf School of English's Robert Haiduke Poetry Contest. She lives in Dedham, MA, with her husband, son, daughter and cat. Please find out more about Caitlin's work here: www.caitlintdrobinson.com.

SETH ROSENBLOOM is a poet and consultant to companies on leadership and management. His poems have recently appeared in *On The Seawall, Ilanot Review* and *Midway Journal,* and other publications. His poetry has been nominated for Best of the Net and has been a finalist for the Tom Howard/ Margaret Reid Poetry Prize. Seth grew-up near Washington DC and lives in Seattle.

JOCELYN ROYALTY is a recent graduate from the creative writing program at the University of Maine at Farmington. Previously, she attended the ACES Educational Center for the Arts in New Haven, Connecticut. She has interned at the *Yale Alumni Magazine, Rustica,* and the Burlington Writer's Workshop. Her work has most recently appeared in the *Oyster River Pages, The Rockvale Review, Club Plum, Allegheny Review,* and *Okay Donkey.*

KATHY SHORR is winner of the 2024 Joe Gouveia Outermost Poetry Contest. She grew up in Ohio and Tennessee, but has lived for a long time near the tip of Cape Cod. She received an MFA in writing from Vermont College. Recent poems have appeared or are forthcoming in the *Atlanta Review, Cape Cod Poetry Review, Pangyrus,* and *Loch Raven Review,* and on the Passager Books podcast *Burning Bright.*

ELI SLOVER serves as a poetry reader for West Trade Review. Their poetry appears in *Gyroscope Review, Frost Meadow Review, MAYDAY Magazine,* and elsewhere.

DONNA SPRUIJT-METZ's books are *To Phrase a Prayer for Peace* (Wildhouse Publishing, 2025), *General Release from the Beginning of the World* (Free Verse Editions, 2023) and *Scuttle My Balloon* (with Flower Conroy, Pictureshow Press 2025) and her translation from the Dutch of Lucas Hirsch's 'Wu Wei Eats an Egg' (Ben Yehuda Press 2025). Chapbooks include *Slippery Surfaces, And Haunt the World* (with Flower Conroy) and *Dear Ghost* (winner Harbor Review Editor's prize). Her poems appear in *Poem-a-day, Alaska Quarterly Review, American Poetry Review* and elsewhere. She's an emeritus professor, MacDowell fellow, rabbinical school drop-out, and former classical flutist. She gets restless. Read her work at donnasmetz.com.

SUSAN SOLOMON is a freelance paintress living in the beautiful Twin Cities area of Minneapolis/Saint Paul. Her website is susansolomonpainter.com

MEGHAN STERLING (she/her/hers) is a Maine writer whose work is published in *Los Angeles Review, Colorado Review, Rhino Poetry, Hunger Mountain* and many other journals. Her books include *Self-Portrait with Ghosts of the Diaspora* (Harbor Editions), *Comfort the Mourners* (Everybody Press) and *View from a Borrowed Field* (Lily Poetry Review's 2022 Paul Nemser Book Prize winner.) Her latest collection, *You Are Here to Break Apart* was published by Lily in 2025. Read her work at meghansterling.com.

JW SUMMERISLE is an autistic poet from the English East Midlands. once commended by and once a winner of the Foyles Young Poets of the Year Award. They have two chapbooks in print: *kinfolk with black sunflowers poetry press,* (2022) and *the book of bad mothers* (2024) with Back Room Poetry. They have a forthcoming book from Alien Buddha Press called *Prayer for the Uninitiated.*

KAREEM TAYYAR is the author of *Keats in San Francisco & Other Poems* (nd his work has2022) appeared in *Poetry Magazine, Prairie Schooner,* and *Alaska Quarterly Review.* His poem, "Two Poets," received the 2022 *Atlanta Review* International Poetry Prize, and his novel, *The Prince of Orange County* received the 2020 Eric Hoffer Prize for Young Adult Fiction. In 2020 he was awarded a Glenna Luschei Poetry Prize, and in 2019,he was a recipient of a Wurlitzer Poetry Fellowship.

PETER URKOWITZ lives in Salem, Massachusetts, where he works in a college library. He was drawn to the local poetry scene as a spectator and began writing his own work. He has published poems in *Meat for Tea: The Valley Review* and in *Oddball Magazine*. He is the author of *Fake Zodiac Signs: An Astro-Illogical Guidebook*.

ANASTASIA VASSOS' poems have been nominated for the Pushcart Prize, Best of the Net, and Best New Poets. She is the author of *Nostos* (2023) and *Nike Adjusting Her Sandal* (2021). Find her work in *RHINO, Whale Road Review, Thrush, Comstock Review, Lily Poetry Review,* and elsewhere. She speaks three languages and rides her bicycle in Boston. The Atlantic is the ocean she loves best.

SHANNON K. WINSTON is the author of *The Worry Dolls* (Glass Lyre Press, 2025) and *The Girl Who Talked to Paintings* (Glass Lyre Press, 2021). Her individual poems have appeared in *Bracken, Cider Press Review, Los Angeles Review, RHINO, Poetry, SWWIM Every Day, West Trestle Review,* and elsewhere. She holds an MFA from the Warren Wilson Program for Writers and lives in Bloomington, IN.

WENDY WISNERis the author of three books of poems, most recently *The New Life,* published by Cornerstone Press (University of Wisconsin Stevens-Point) and named a finalist for the Foreword INDIES Book of the Year. Wendy's poems and essays have appeared in *Prairie Schooner, Spoon River Review, Bellevue Literary Review, The Washington Post, Lilith Magazine,* and elsewhere.